"Paranormal is Normal, Supernatural is Natural, Just Not Yet Understood"

"Terms and Expressions used in researching the Paranormal and the Supernatural"

By

Cynthia Miller Kreiner

Dedication to my parents Ernie and Inez, my daughter Kennedy and husband Pete. Thank you for your never ending love and support. Remember!!!

Acknowledgments

No Boundaries Paranormal

Front cover graphic – Roland Saenz Jr.

Back cover graphic – Joedy Cook

References from Wikipedia www.wikipedia.org

Introduction

This book started in a spiral notebook of notes I took when I began investigating many years ago. People would ask when I would say EVP, Mel Meter, K2... what is that? I would use terms like Anomaly, portal, spirit... again what is that? Then in my lectures I would talk about my gift and having been born with a Caul... what is a Caul? Then I would be asked about Michael the Archangel, Gabriel, Mothman, Sasquatch, Jersey Devil, Demons...

Who are they?

Then one day I was talking with my Dad about what I was doing in the paranormal field, he and my mom are so supportive of anything us kids do, but again they didn't understand the terms I used is describing what I was doing. A light went on... Take your notes and turn it into something to help people understand that the

"Paranormal is Normal, Supernatural is Natural, Just Not Yet Understood"

This was put together as an aid in the basic understanding of parapsychology, paranormal research and the ghost-hunting techniques. This is research I have done on my own to educate myself in understanding the Terminology and Expressions used in Paranormal Research and more. This by no means is a complete list of Paranormal Terminology and Expressions.

Content

About the Author

Cynthia (Cindy) Miller Kreiner

"Cindy is not a Ghost Hunter, she knows they exist" She is a paranormal researcher from Michigan, USA.

She is a mom to a beautiful daughter Kennedy, who is number one in her life and wife to a very patient loving husband Pete. Both are very supportive of all she does.

Other than family, many are just finding out what she does and "Her Gift". It just wasn't something talked about.

Cindy is embracing every moment while on her adventures. Her goal is to help people understand that the paranormal is normal. It has become a passion of hers and a drive for her to help everyday people, friends, families, and children (and wishing she had this kind of help when she was a child, it just wasn't talked about) to understand the existence of the paranormal by investigating the scientific aspects of the paranormal and putting her abilities to use. The paranormal has always been a part of Cindy's life since she can remember. Cindy helps children who have signs of being gifted, for them to understand they are not alone, not to be scared, and that they have been given a gift. She will keep pushing the limits even further as she adventures off into new, unknown, dark places. Cindy's quest is to research and study what else is out there beyond the realm in which we all live.

Cindy has had the pleasure to work on cold cases with Homicide Task Force to find answers for the cases brought to her.

One of her experiences has been documented in a book written by author Kim Cool called Haunted Theatres of Southwest Florida.

Founder of No Boundaries Paranormal

Terms and Expressions

-A-

Abacomancy - (from the Greek amathos, for sand), is an art and practice where your fortune can be told by reading the patterns in dust, dirt, silt, sand, or the ashes of the deceased. Reading the patterns is believed to give some insight into the future. Readers drop the dirt, sand, or ashes on a flat surface and start looking for a pattern that may represent symbols or pictures. Some look for certain symbols that are seen over and over. This art and practice has been dated back as the twelfth and thirteenth centuries.

Abductee - is a human being that is forced from terrestrial surroundings to an apparent alien space craft against his or her will as in kidnapping. Someone who claims to had an experience of being abducted, abduction by extraterrestrials.

Abduction - The act in which a human being that is forced into an apparent alien space craft against his or her will as in kidnapping. One is taken apparently by extraterrestrials.

Abominable Snowman - is a creature usually described as a shaggy man-beast that is only ever briefly seen moving across snow swept landscapes, leaving behind very large footprints.

Abracadabra - Originally a Kabbalistic charm. Magicians in modern times used as a popular magical incantation. A magician will use this today to add mystery to their performance. Abracadabra was used to heal fevers and forms of inflammation.

Absent Healing - is a form of healing that takes place when the person giving the healing is not in direct contact with the person to be healed.

Absent sitter - is someone who has readings done about them while they are not present.

ABSM - An ABSM could be any of a variety of reported hairy bipeds from around the world. Although the term is derived from Abominable Snowman, it is considered a less sensational alternative.

Absolute Energy - An invisible primal life force found in the atmosphere, necessary for the existence of all life in the universe.

Absolute Humidity - The amount of water vapor present in a unit volume of air

Activity - conscious and unconscious thoughts have an effect on outer manifestations this effect corresponds to the type and kind of thought.

Acheri- According to Indian lore, plagued demons and spirits that appear as gray skinned small girl. They live on mountain tops and come into villages to spread diseases by infecting them, mostly to children. It known to cast its shadow on those it wishes to infect.

Acupressure - A Chinese and Japanese treatment by applying pressure to certain points on the body.

Acupuncture - An alternative medicine discipline that works by stimulating certain points of the body with thin needles for therapeutic purposes or to relieve pain or produce regional anesthesia.

Adamastor - The name of a spirit inhabiting the Cape of Good Hope, which prophesizes doom for those sailing beyond the cape towards India.

Adept - a person "The Skilled One" "Mastery of Psychic Powers" who is considered well versed or highly skilled in a particular discipline. In occult practices it can refer to someone who has achieved true enlightenment, a particular stage of initiation, or level of expertise in magic.

Adhesion - When two non-conducting materials hold onto their electric charge.

Adjuration - A formula used by conjurers and exorcists dealing with evil spirits. The spirit is commanded in the name of the Christian God to obey the conjurer/exorcist.

Adytum - A Greek word describing the most holy part of a temple. In occultism it describes the most holy area of an initiation center, the most sacred or reserved part of any place of worship.

Aeromancy - the art of foretelling the future by the observation of atmospheric, air or sky phenomena. This goes beyond the range of weather prognostications, concentrating in such things as wind currents, cloud shape and formation, comets and falling stars, spectral formations, and other phenomena which are not normally seen or visible in the heavens.

Aetities - A stone said to be found in the throat or stomach of an eagle. It is supposed to heal falling sickness and prevent untimely birth.

Afrit - this is a very dangerous demon according to an Arabian legend. It was once the spirit of a murdered man, who now seeks to avenge his death. The demon's spirit is supposed to rise up from the body of the murdered man. It appears as smoke at the spot that the murder took place.

After-Death World - Umbrella term, any level of the etheric word that is alive, vibrating and full of soul-minds without physical bodies.

Afterlife - a life or existence believed to follow death. It can also be life at a later time but usually after death. Afterlife is known as the Other Side, the Great Beyond, and Heaven or Hell, as well as many other names. Basically, it's the life after this one we're in now. Every culture on the planet has some idea or belief in an afterlife, and what it is like. Some believe that we are reborn, to lead out another form of life on the planet. Others believe that the next life is much the same as it is now, with the same family life and there is enough for all. There is a belief in tribal systems of the Underworld. The place is under the earth and the spirits of the dead live together in villages.

Age of Aquarius - Usually refers to the end of an era and the beginning of another, 'the end of times' or the dawning of a 'new world order'.

Agent - A living person who is the focus of poltergeist activity, investigation in a psychokinesis experiment, or person who tries to communicate or impart information to another via telepathy or some similar means. It can also be used to describe the force causing a haunting. Similarly the word describes the person communicating information in an ESP experiment. Very often this is a person of teen years.

Agogwe - The Agogwe are little, human-like, hairy, bipeds reported consistently from the forests of Eastern Africa.

Agriglyph - is a large design created in a field of vegetation by pressing down parts of the growth. The term is an alternative to Crop Circles. It was introduced to reflect the higher complexity of many such anomalies.

Ahool - Giant unknown bats are reported to reside in a region of western Java, plus similar reports under different names from Vietnam and the Philippines; possibly known as Orang-bati in Seram, Indonesia.

Akasha - It is believed by many modern Pagans that the Akasha, Spirit, is the Fifth Element. It has been said that Akasha is the spiritual force that Earth, Air, Fire, and Water descend from. Some also believe that the combination of the four elements make up that which is Akasha, and that Akasha exists in every living creature in existence, without Akasha, there is no spirit, no soul, and no magic. Theosophists believe that persons with special psychic powers can tap into the Akasha or "Astral Light".

Akashic Records - Memories of all experiences catalogued since the beginning of time, believed by some mystical doctrines to be stored permanently in a spiritual substance (Akasha). A spiritual library of all deeds and acts. Some people claim to have been able to visit and browse them during meditation. Theosophists to contain records that persons such as clairvoyants or spiritual beings can tap into. They do this by using their "astral bodies" or "astral senses" to gain access to these stored spiritual insights.

Alastor - A demon in Roman mythology, the evil genius of a house.

Alberich - In Scandinavian mythology, is the King of the Dwarves.

Alchemist - A scientist who studies how to transmute anything from a lower form to a higher form using both a chemical process and a spiritual process.

Alchemy - The Science of turning the baser metals into gold or silver by chemical means. The byproduct, "Quicksilver," was thought to have magical powers. This was a very perfected science in Egyptian times and lasted all the way up into the 14th-16th Century A.D. when some of the alchemy methods were lost due to wars and fires that were amid in those times.

Aleuromacy - The art of using flour. In one technique, sentences are written on pieces of paper, rolled up in flour and distributed amongst participants to tell them their future. Another method involves reading the residue left in a flour/water container.

Alectromancy - The art of using a cock or hen. The bird is placed in the center of a circle surrounded by letters. The bird indicates letters which spell out answers to questions.

Aliens - are creatures, or beings that allegedly come from outer space possibly from other planets, galaxies, universes or even different dimensions. They are sometimes referred to as extra-terrestrials.

Alien Abduction - a form of abduction or kidnapping by aliens (beings from another world), or extraterrestrial beings, usually an unpleasant experience, often involving painful procedures.

All Hallows Eve (Halloween) - The night of October 31st is originally a Pagan festival of darkness, and death. Halloween was believed to be the one time of year when the souls of the dead revisited their former homes. The Celts started it. The Celts had their New Year celebration on November 1st, which was called Samhain. This means "end of summer". This celebrated day was for the Lord of the Dead. It was believed that on the night before November 1st, the mystical veil between the world of the living and the world of the dead was at its thinnest. Communication between the living and dead, therefore, was much easier on this night. During the night, the Celts believed that the dead would rise up from their graves to cause a little trouble in the neighborhood. It was also believed that the Lord of the Dead would gather up the lost souls and re-sentences them to either a year in animal form (this was for the ones that were bad) or another year of death (that was for the good boys and girls). The villagers would make offerings to the Lord of the Dead so he'd be a little nicer to the lost souls. The Celts also dressed up in costumes to confuse the spirits. The modern use of wearing costumes originated from the use of scary masks worn to scare the roaming souls away. The Christians made changes and now it is known today as Halloween.

All Saints Day - November 1, is the day the Catholic Church honors its saints. The day is said to be special for the spirit world and paranormal activity as well.

All Soul's Day - The anniversary of Siddhartha's death celebrated in respect of all people who have made their transition.

Almas - a creature reported to be of ape-like appearance that inhabits the mountains in central Asia, which was up until a few years ago part of the Soviet Union.

Alomancy - The art of using salt in a similar way to aleuromancy.

Alpha Rhythm/Alpha Waves - A pattern of electrical activity in the brain of somebody awake but relaxed or drowsy, registering on an electroencephalograph at a reading between 8 and 13 hertz. Some people feel that many psychics get in to an 'alpha state' to work.

Alphitomancy - A method of judging a person's innocence or guilt by feeding them a specially-prepared barley loaf. If the accused suffers from stomach irritation or pain, they are deemed guilty.

Altered State of Consciousness - A term used to refer to any state of consciousness that is different from normal states of waking or sleeping that most of us experience. ASCs include hypnosis, trance, ecstasy, and meditative states that may produce euphoria. ASCs do not necessarily have anything at all to do with paranormal or psychic ability.

Ampere - A unit of electric current strength, equal to a flow of one coulomb per second.

Amperes Per Meter (A/m) - Used to measure the magnetic field in relation to electric current.

Amorphous - Matter or energy that has no definitive shape or form.

Amulet - This refers to just about anything one believes to hold some magic power for protection against things like ghosts, demons, or just about any evil there is. Most are made of jewelry, gold, silver or gems. Necklaces with runes carved into them and religious items to be worn to either bring good luck or to ward off evil.

Analgesia - Insensibility to pain most common among mediums and holy men.

Ancestor Worship - A religious practice which involves the honoring and veneration of ancestors. They are worshiped as deities. In some cases family will put out food and drink for the dead in the belief that the ancestral spirits will bring good fortune to the family and will protect them from evil.

Ancestral Being - are spirit entities from the early days of the world, according to the Dreamtime or Creation myths of Australia's aboriginal tribes. Modern science dismisses these ideas as purely the stuff of fantasy but many aboriginals firmly believe in their continued existence.

Ancestral Ghost - A discarnate being that communicates or makes his presence known to an earthling who is capable of psychism.

Ancestral Spirit - An ancient spirit that follows families or certain groups of families to where ever they move. These spirits are said to watch and protect over the families, and often can give forewarnings of tragedies and deaths. Throughout history historic and royal families have claimed to have such connections.

Ancient Anomalies - are ancient artifacts which just don't appear to fit in with the accepted view of archaeology or history. For example in Antelope Spring in Utah a 500 million year old fossil has been found which is said to reveal a trilobite crushed by a sandaled foot. Archaeology suggests that man was not walking the earth at this time let alone wearing sandals hence the anomaly.

Ancient Astronauts - Extraterrestrial beings that are said to have visited Earth in the distant past were helping early humans develop culture and technology.

Andean Wolf - These unrecognized mountain dogs are seen in South America.

Anemometer - Device that notes or measures the wind speed or velocity. It is a common weather station instrument.

Angel - A spiritual being, an instrument of divine justice, more powerful than a human, a spiritual being that does the work of God. They are the "middle-man" between the living and God. The word "Angel" comes from the Greek words angelos, meaning "messenger. This is the primary job of the angel, going back and forth from earth to heaven. They bring prayers up and answer back down. It is also their job to act out the will of God, whether it is to help the living or punish them. Although the ideas that inspired the concept of angels, they are pretty much specific to Christian, Judaism and Islamic religions. They are most often described as very clean and wearing white robes. They have large wings of white feathers and are usually male. Another description is that of the "Mysterious Person." This is a person who shows up during a crisis situation and offers very good advice to help someone out. After the situation is under control, the Mystery Man is nowhere to be found. This leads many to the belief that it was an angel who stepped in to help.

Angelic Host - A group of synchronized etheric world intelligences desiring to offer assistance to civilization.

Angel Magic - Since man has held a belief in angels he has also tried to harness their help and power for his own ends. There are generally two ways in which believers try to do this and these methods are called evocation or invocations.

Angelolatry - a term used to describe the veneration or worship of angels.

Angelology - is a term used to describe the study or science of angels.

Angelophany - is a term used to describe the visible or otherwise tangible manifestation of angels to human beings.

Animal magnetism - A supposed type of magnetism between living beings. Some claim that this force can be transmitted between people to help with healing.

Animal Mutilation - a term which refers to cases of animal corpses (usually cattle), which have been found with strange injuries. These injuries are often difficult to explain in terms of accident, predators and illness. Often the corpse has missing body parts (e.g. genitals), has been drained of blood and many injuries appear to have been carried out with surgical precision.

Animal Psi - The apparent ability of animals to exhibit psychic powers such as clairvoyance, telepathy and even psychokinesis. Reported examples include the ability to sense impending danger, to sense the proximity of an owner, to sense harm to an owner at a distance, and to navigate unknown territory.

Animism - a belief in the existence of individual spirits that inhabit natural objects and all living things, a belief that everything possesses a spiritual essence or soul. The word is derived from the Latin "anima", meaning soul. It can also be the belief in the existence of spiritual beings that are separable or separate from bodies. Alternatively animism is the hypothesis that an immaterial force animates the universe.

Anima Mundi - An ancient Latin term meaning "The Soul of the World".

Animism - This is the name given to the belief systems of tribal societies around the world, a belief in the existence of individual spirits that inhabit natural objects and all living things, a belief that everything possesses a spiritual essence or soul.

Anniversary Imprint - A spirit or haunting that seems most active during a specific calendar period (day, week, month, etc.). This date may coincide with known dates of a death or other eventful emotional discharges associated with dead entities during their human lifetimes.

Announcing Dream - a dream that is believed to signal the rebirth of an individual.

Anomaly - Something that deviates from the considered "normal." That which is not easily classified, something that is unusual or unexpected.

Anomalous Cognition - a form of information transfer by an unknown means and without sensorial stimuli. Some individuals are able to gain access to this information, but the process is not yet understood. The term anomalous cognition is also known as remote viewing, clairvoyance, but more generally replaces the term of ESP.

Anomalous Experience - is an umbrella term for types of strange or weird experiences which science does not yet fully understand or cannot yet explain.

Anomalous Perturbation - another term for psychokinesis.

Anomalous Phenomena - strange naturally occurring phenomena that science cannot yet define or explain.

Anthropomorphize - Anthropomorphism is the attribution of human characteristics to, or, some would argue, recognition of human characteristics in, non-human creatures and beings, phenomena, material states and objects or abstract concepts. Examples include animals and plants and forces of nature such as winds, rain or the sun depicted as creatures with human motivation able to reason and converse.

Anti-gravity - A hypothetical device or force which is immune to the effects of gravity. Various claims have been made about the invention of such devices but none have ever been reliably demonstrated.

Antichrist - The demon that is predicted to precede the Second Coming of Christ, in Revelation 13.

Apparition - A manifestation of a person, animals or objects. Spirits are apparitions of dead people. There are many different kinds of apparitions, but the most widely known form is that of seeing a figure that appears to be transparent. It's believed that they are projected images, brought about by the energy stored in the area. Others believe they are the personality of a deceased person and can still interact with the living.

Apparition Color Correspondences - It's believed that the color of apparitions is associated with the person when they were alive.

1. Black - Religious devotee such as a priest, monk or nun.

2. Blue - Usually associated with the American Union Army or the spirit of someone who died in a tragic love affair or while depressed.

3. Gray - Usually associated with the American Confederate Army or the spirit in a library in America. In other countries, the color characterizes people who died tragically for the sake of love or died while brokenhearted.

4. Green - Someone of Irish heritage.

5. Orange - Someone who wishes to be noticed.

6. Pink - The spirit of a person who committed suicide because they could not be with their lover.

7. Purple - A friendly spirit.

8. Red - The spirit of a very passionate or flirtatious person.

9. White - Innocence.

10. Yellow - The spirit of a very opinionated person.

Apport - An object or living being that materializes from thin air in the presence of a medium. Often claimed to be a gift from the spirits.

Aquamarine - Used to purify the body before ritual, as a protective amulet when travelling over water, to sooth emotional problems, and to enhance the use of psychic powers.

Arabhar - These unconfirmed flying snakes are located in the Arabian Sea region.

Ararat Anomaly -The Ararat Anomaly is a large object (over 100 meters in length) photographed on Mount Ararat in Turkey. Some people believe it is Noah's Ark.

Arkeology - Is the search for the physical remains of Noah's Ark.

Arcanum - Something hidden. The plural arcana refer to the varied knowledge of occult lore. It is also used to describe the 22 picture cards of the tarot card pack.

Arch-Angels - Etheric world intelligences that have purified their soul-minds from all imperfection before earth came into being.

1. Michael - It is generally thought that Michael is foremost among angels. He is considered to be of the class of seraphim and also known as the angel of the burning bush through which God spoke to Moses. He ranks as the highest of the host regardless of which major faith is being followed and also appears in the book of Daniel, where God states him as being the highest within the angelic ranks. He was responsible not only for fighting and enchaining Satan during the war, but he also leads the celestial armies. Although classed as the chief angel Michael also heads up other ranks within the hierarchy.

2. Gabriel - Is probably most well-known for the Annunciation where he told Mary of the impending birth of Christ. Generally Gabriel is seen as a slightly more benevolent spirit than his ally Michael. He

was also the messenger that brought news of the coming birth of John the Baptist and appeared to Zacharias.

3. Raphael - Is considered the head of the guardian angels. Although the ranking of chief of virtues is sometimes given to Michael it is generally attributed to Raphael. He is a seraph but Raphael is also mentioned as being a member of the cherubim, dominations and powers. He is known for teaching Solomon how to bind demons into slave labor when Solomon's Temple was being built and also teaching Noah how to construct the ark before the flood.

4. Uriel - Is one of the most dedicated and faithful members of the host and as such was put in charge of Tartarus (another name for Hades), He Identified as both a seraph and a cherub and is most well-known for his appearance in the book of Revelation where he calls forth the birds of the air to feast upon the fallen. Here his role was as Regent of the Sun. Although Raphael is credited with teaching the building of the ark, Uriel warned Noah of the impending flood. He also attacked Moses for failing to circumcise his son.

5. Chamuel - Is considered along with Gabriel to be one of the comforting angels of Jesus when he was in Gethsemane. Although considered a chief domination, he is also a member of the order of powers. Some believe Chamuel to be the angel who wrestled with Jacob and damaged Jacob's thigh.

6. Jophiel - Is accredited for his role in driving Adam and Eve from the Garden of Eden after they ate the forbidden fruit. Should this be the case then Jophiel also gains the honor of being the first angel mentioned in the Bible. Jophiel is a cherubim.

7. Zadkiel - Is believed by some to be chief, considered an angel of mercy he belongs to the ranks of the dominions. Zadkiel is the patron angel of all who forgive as well as the angel of freedom mercy and benevolence.

8. Raguel - Has the honor of ensuring the good behavior of the other angels. He is of the principalities and needs to be vigilant.

9. Remiel - Has two main responsibilities. Firstly he is the angel that acts as the guide for souls of the faithful after being weighed by Michael at the last trump. Such a role such a role leads to the assumption that Ramiel is a power.

10. Sariel - Is believed to be an angel of knowledge who works alongside of Raguel. He is a seraph whose role is to decide the fate of angels which stray from God's path. He is also one of the leaders in Heaven's armies and his name is written upon the shields of one of the fighting forces.

11. Raziel - Is a cherubim and ranked as the special patron to the first human. He like Sariel is also an angel of knowledge. He is the giver of divine mysteries.

Area 51 - Popular name for part of a secret military base in North America, approximately 95 miles north of Las Vegas, rumored to be home to research involving extraterrestrial beings and/or technology.

Area 54 - Part of Area 51, rumored to be the location of secret aircraft tests.

Ariolater - A person who foretells the future by interpreting omens.

Artefact - is a term used in parapsychology to describe evidence of supernatural phenomena that is not genuine, faked or that has been falsified by purely normal means.

ASC (Altered State of Consciousness) - a brain state differing from normal consciousness. Sometimes associated with the transportation to a higher realm of consciousness or mystical experience. Feelings experienced during an altered brain state can be both pleasant and unpleasant.

Ascendant - The degree of the Zodiac which is nearest the eastern horizon at the time of a person's birth.

Aset Ka - A spiritual society and metaphysical order of mysteries.

Aspects - In astrology, a large number of angular relationships between planets and other nodal points.

Asport - An object or living being that vanishes from a location. Can be considered the opposite of an apport.

ASQ - The three phases of an EVP investigation (Alone, Supervise, Question): 1. Leave the recorder alone until the tape runs out 2. Supervise the recording area while it records 3. Ask questions to check for an intelligent haunting; (Also: ASA - Alone, Supervise, Ask).

Astragalomancy - A method of by throwing dice or bones in which letters are marked on the faces of the dice or bones and the future is foretold from the words formed as they fall.

Astral Body - The invisible spirit of a person (or, more unlikely, animal). Out of body experience and at death also known as the KA. The ethereal duplicate of the physical body.

Astral Plane - The level of existence through which spirits of the dead first pass. The level in which an Astrally projected spirit travels.

Astral Projection - The separation of the astral body (or spirit) from the physical body. The astral body travels in the astral plane to locations near or far.

Astral Spirit - the word astral on its own means relating to, resembling or emanating from the stars. Astral spirits are those formerly thought to inhabit heavenly or celestial objects for example stars or planets. Astral spirits in the Middle Ages were represented as spirits of the dead, spirits that originated in fire and also as fallen angels.

Astral Travel - Astral projection (or astral travel) is an interpretation of any form of out-of-body experience (OBE) that assumes the existence of an "astral body" separate from the physical body and capable of travelling outside it. Astral projection or travel denotes the astral body leaving the physical body to travel in the astral plane.

Astrology - A science and art that brings guidance and counsel to mankind based on one's birth date.

Atavism - The term atavism (derived from the Latin atavus, a great-grandfather's grandfather; more generally, an ancestor) denotes the tendency to revert to ancestral type. An atavism is an evolutionary throwback, such as traits reappearing which had disappeared generations ago. Atavisms occur because genes for previously existing phenotypical features are often preserved in DNA, even though the genes are not expressed in some or most of the organisms possessing them.

Athame - A black handled cleansed and consecrated ceremonial double-edged dagger, one of several magical tools used in New Age Witchcraft (Wicca). The knife is never used for blood-letting, and rarely used to cut.

Atlantis - A mythological continent said to have existed thousands of years ago and inhabited by advanced civilizations. It is said to have been destroyed in an unknown cataclysm.

Atmospheric Apparition - Not actually a ghost or spirit, but instead a "visual imprint" of people and events that was left behind in the environment and continues to replay.

Attached Spirit (attachment) - Is when a spirit is attracted to a living person because of some connection to the person, either emotionally, similar life-experiences, or the spirit could have known the person in life or even a past life. And then begins to coexist within the living person. After a while, the spirit and/or the person they "attached" to finds that they've become emotionally attached. Often the person will feel safe or even complacent about the spirit being with them.

Auditory - Of or relating to the sense, organs, or experience of hearing.

Audio - Audio is an important part to a successful investigation. Come equipped with sound recorders, talk boxes and digital repeaters. These items play a vital part in communicating with spirits. Many times spirit voices will be picked up on audio recorders which are called EVPs.

Augur - A diviner or soothsayer.

Augury - an event that is experienced as indicating important things to come; an omen or sign that something is coming; "he hoped it was an augury"; "it was a sign from God". It also means a prediction, prognostication and indication of the future. For example "the man had an augury of his future greatness". As a verb augury is an art or practice of divination. It can be the art or practice of foretelling events by observing the actions of birds etc.; as mentioned above a practice sometimes known as divination.

Aura - Bands of colored lights that surround a body (field of energy) that represent the emotional state of the being. Believed to be seen by clairvoyants and sensitives.

Aura Cleansing - A metaphysical ritual that clears an aura of all negative energies which may attract negative spirits.

Austromancy - Another word for Aeromancy.

Automatic Writing - The production of written material by a spirit through a person but without conscious control of that person. Often, a person may write pages and pages of words that, upon "awakening", they do not remember writing.

Automatism - An unconscious or involuntary muscular movement caused by spirits.

Autoscopy - The visual hallucination or image of one's body looking back at themselves from a position outside the body.

Avatar - Refers to a deliberate descent of a deity from heaven to earth, and is mostly translated into English as "incarnation", but more accurately as "appearance" or "manifestation".

Ba - a concept originating from the ancient Egyptians, ba is not dissimilar to the modern concept of a soul, the supersensible part of a person's essence that is believed to be immortal.

Backward blessing - The practice of reciting the Lord's Prayer backwards, said to invoke the Devil.

Ball Lightning - A rare form of lightning in the shape of a glowing red ball that can last anywhere from a few seconds to several minutes. Typically associated with Thunderstorms, these spheres are thought to consist of ionized gas.

Banishing - Ceremonial procedure used to cast an unwanted energy or beings from a person(s) or place.

Banshee - A wailing spirit or "death omen" that will appear to be in two different places at the same time.

Baphomet - is an imagined pagan deity, (i.e., a product of Christian folklore concerning pagans) revived in the 19th century as a figure of Satanism. It first appeared in a late 12th-century Provençal poem as a corruption of "Muhammad", but later it appeared as a term for a pagan idol in trial transcripts of the Inquisition of the Knights Templar in the early 1300s. However, in the 19th century the name came into popular English-speaking consciousness with the publication of various works of pseudo-history that tried to link the Knights Templar with conspiracy theories elaborating on their suppression. The name Baphomet then became associated with a "Sabbatic Goat" image drawn by Eliphas Lévi.

Bardo - is an intermediate state of existence that usually refers to a state between life and rebirth. The term has its roots in Tibetan Buddhism.

Barghest - A large black dog apparition considered a harbinger of doom.

Barmanu - Reportedly strong, muscular, and hairy humanoids reported from the Shishi-kuh valley in Pakistan.

Barometer - Measures the atmospheric pressure on water, air or mercury. Standard barometers consist of a glass tube of about thirty inches in height, closed at one end with liquid mercury resting inside. High pressures force the mercury column higher while decreased pressures lower the mercury level. Higher temperatures can affect the density of the liquid mercury but the scale reflects this possible environmental deviation. One atmospheric unit is equivalent to 29.9 inches or 760 millimeters of mercury.

Basic Technique - A test for clairvoyance where the subject guesses what a card is.

Basilisk - Mythical king of reptiles, said to kill with a glance.

Battlefield Ghosts - These are places with great violence, trauma and intense emotion are typically subject to hauntings. There are no places more violent than battlefields, and it is rare to hear of a battlefield that isn't haunted. Most battlefield hauntings are residual hauntings where fragments of the battle are replayed over and over again. Other hauntings are from spirits who have not crossed over, most likely because they feel they can't due to the nature of their death. Some believe retro-cognition is also an element in battlefield hauntings.

Bat Man - is a bat winged humanoid and a phenomenon that comes from the Russian Far East around the Primorskiy Kray Territory. A hunter called A.I. Kurentsov spotted the beast several years ago in the immense taiga forest as it flew over his fire. The bat man or letayuschiy chelovek, which translates, as 'flying human' is also famed for its eerie cry, likened to a woman's scream but ending in a 'lugubrious howl'.

Battery - Investigations usually take six to eight hours so it is imperative to have extra batteries to maintain your equipment power levels. Also, there is the possibility of battery drain which occasionally occurs paranormally. It is best to prepare for every contingency.

Beast of Bodmin Moor - is a black panther like creature that is believed to inhabit Bodmin Moor in Cornwall. Indeed there have been around 60 other big cat sightings recorded in the area since 1983 and experts believe there is a population of big cats in and around mid-Cornwall. There have even been some sightings as far apart as Kent and Scotland.

Beast of Gévaudan - was described as being a huge wolf-like beast, which killed its victims 'by savagely tearing out their throats before devouring their bodies or simply ripping them apart'. The beast came to public attention between June 1764 and June 1767 when a large number of murders (mainly women and children) occurred in Gévaudan, a place situated in the district of Lozère in south-eastern France.

Beelzebub - One of Satan's chief Lieutenants, considered Satan's "left hand man".

Belphegor - The Moabitish god of licentiousness and orgies. In medieval times, the name given to a devil.

Benign Spirit - A spirit that is not harmful.

Bennington Triangle - A wilderness area in Vermont, USA, where a number of people have mysteriously disappeared.

Bergman's Bear - Possible unknown species of giant bear once roamed Eastern Asia, and still may.

Bermuda Triangle - An area in the Atlantic Ocean boundary by Bermuda, Florida and Puerto Rico. Various paranormal events have been reported from the area, in particular, a number of missing planes and sea vessels.

Bicorn - A mythical creature said to grow fat on the flesh of devoted husbands. A female bicorn is known as a chichevache.

Bigfoot - One of many names given to a legendary ape-like creature said to live in the wilderness of North America. Bigfoot is generally regarded as the USA version of Sasquatch (Canada) and Yeti (Nepal).

Bili Ape - Giant chimpanzees appear to live in remote east Africa, where much evidence points to their existence, including photos, footprints and ground nests.

Billet Reading - is a procedure that involves placing a secretly written question on a piece of paper. This paper is then folded and sealed up inside an envelope and then given to a psychic, who then attempts to answer the question contained within.

Bilocation - The appearance of a person in two distant places simultaneously. Some believe that those they describe as ascended masters may have been able to have been not only at two places at once but to have been in control of more than one soul at a time.

Biofeedback - A general techniques that involve giving person information about their current physiological state (EG. heart rate, EEG). Biofeedback is used to enable people to control consciously their own physiological autonomic processes.

Bio-PK - Psycho kinetic effects on biological processes. The fabled ability of being able to do such things as encourage rapid plant growth or increase a person's heart rate for example.

Birds-of-Paradise - Six species from New Guinea and surrounding islands, and a distinctive Long-Tailed Black Bird-of-Paradise from Goodenough Island are of interest to cryptozoology.

Birth stones - A series of stones linked to the 12 zodiac signs.

Black Art - To deliberately use psychic energy for evil intent.

Black Magic - The practice of conjuring preternatural forces for a specific evil purpose.

Black Mass - The mass said in honor of Satan at the black witches Sabbath and by Satanists.

Black Panthers and Manned Mystery Cats - Sighting of large Black Panthers and seemingly "African Lions" with manes in the Midwest USA have law enforcement officials on the alert.

Blind Trial - An experimental control group in which subjects are not privy to certain key features pertaining to the experiment. Also used to refer to a procedure where a judge is asked to compare targets and responses without knowing which responses were made to which targets.

Blue Mountain panthers - These unknown cats reportedly live in the Blue Mountains of the east coast of Australia in the state of New South Wales.

Blue Tiger - These mystery felids are spotted in the Fujian Province, China, and are also filed under the name Black Tiger.

Bobo - Sea monsters of the North Pacific Ocean are frequently reported off Monterey Bay since the 1940s, and have been given this local name.

Bogey (-Man) - The bogeyman (also spelled boogeyman, bogyman, bogyman, boogieman, boogey monster) is a legendary monster. The bogeyman has no specific appearance and conceptions of the monster can vary drastically even from household to household within the same community; in many cases, he simply has no set appearance in the mind of a child, but is just an amorphous embodiment of terror. Bogeyman can be used metaphorically to denote a person or thing of which someone has an irrational fear. Parents often say that if their child is naughty, the bogeyman will get them, in an effort to make them behave. Born with a Veil - A baby born with a thin membrane that envelopes the fetus, it is believed that this child is psychic.

Brimstone - an element that has the properties to burn away negative vibrations and evil spirits.

Brothers of the Shadow - Dark Brothers, Grey Brothers. People who choose to follow the teachings of black magic.

Buffalo Lion - East African mane less lions are said to be man-eaters, and may reflect some new genetic alignments, akin to the King Cheetah discoveries among cheetahs.

Bugaboo - A trickster or prankster ghost.

Bugbear - A terrifying bear apparition that eats children.

Bunyip - Mythological creature from indigenous Australian folklore.

Buru - Fifteen foot long bluish -black giant lizards were seen often in the swamps, lakes and foothills of the Himalayas, up through the 1940s, although they may be extinct now.

Cabinet Manifestation - A box or curtained area in which a physical medium is secured and from which various phenomena may manifest, EG. Lights, objects moving, instruments played). Often the realm of a stage magicians rather than a psychic.

Caddy - These unknown Sea Serpents living off the coast of British Columbia are a popular figure in Canadian cryptozoology.

Caliban - In Shakespeare's The Tempest, the name of a deformed half-human offspring of a devil and a witch.

Call - A call is the response that is made by a subject during a card-guessing test or during any other type of ESP test.

Cambion - Half-human offspring of an incubus and a succubus.

Camera - A device use to capture still images or a sequence of moving images. They operate with the light from the visible, infrared and other electromagnetic spectrums. A basic camera consists of a small opening at one end that allows light to enter, a photosensitive material for recording and a lens for focusing. Photographic film or plates were eventually outmoded through the use of a charge coupled device (CCD) or CMOS sensor. This technology is mainly utilized in most digital cameras used to capture and store images. It is important to recognize shutter speed, flash and brightness of the environment so that one can avoid possible false positives.

Candomble - An African religion mostly practiced in Brazil, although originally confined to the slave population, banned by the Catholic Church, and even criminalized by some governments, Candomble thrived for over four centuries.

Capnomancy - A method of by interpreting patterns of smoke, especially smoke from sacrificial offerings.

Card Guessing - Card guessing is used as an experimental test for ESP in which a subject tries to guess the identity of a set of cards.

Cartomancy - Any method of using playing cards. Tarot is a form of cartomancy.

Case Study - An in-depth investigation of an individual subject.

Caul - A thin membrane of amniotic fluid that remains covering the head of a newborn at birth. Those born with a caul are said to be blessed with luck, protection and supernatural powers. Such individuals are thought to be able to see and speak with ghosts and spirits.

Cerberus - In Greek mythology, a three-headed dog that guards the gate to the infernal regions.

Cerebral Anoxia - Lack of oxygen to the brain, often thought to be responsible for sensory distortions and hallucinations. Sometimes used to explain the effects felt by those who feel they have had a (NDE) near-death experience.

Chain of Being - Originally developed by Plato, a philosophical idea which orders life from the highest spiritual beings to the lowest inanimate objects.

Chakra - A yogic term meaning a series of circular "life force" vortices in a person, at which point energy is received, transformed and distributed.

Chalcedony - A type of translucent quartz, usually a smoky blue in color, which was used by the ancient Egyptians to drive away ghosts, night visions and sadness.

Champ - Giant prehistoric-looking creatures lurk in Lake Champlain, a 109 mile lake that borders New York, Vermont, and Ontario.

Chance - Referred to as Lady Luck, Random, and unpredictable influences on events.

Channeling - In this modern day method of spirit communication, a spirit will pass information directly to a medium or channeler who will then relay the information on to the listener(s).

Channeling - To allow a spirit to enter one's mind and impress thoughts upon the consciousness to be spoken aloud.

Charm - A magical formula recited or sung in order to achieve a desired effect. Sometimes used in the making of amulets and talismans.

Cherub - A member of the second order of etheric world angels, known for their knowledge and help in carrying out the Divine plan.

Chi - Asian term for "Life Force" or biological energy that is inhaled and can be manipulated for specific purposes.

Charge Coupled Device (CCD) - One of the two main types of image sensors used in digital cameras when a picture is taken. The CCD is struck by light coming through the camera's lens; each of the thousands or millions of tiny pixels that make it up converts this light into electrons; the number of electrons, usually described as the pixel's accumulated charge, is measured and then converted to a digital value; this last step occurs outside the device, in a camera component called an analog-to-digital converter.

Charge Imbalance - The static electrical charge created when two adhered no-conductive materials are separated. One becomes positively charged and the other material becomes negatively charged.

Chichevache - A mythical female monster, believed to have subsisted by eating good and virtuous women.

Chimera - In Greek mythology, a beast with a lion's head, goat's body and dragon's tail.

Christian Science - A religious healing movement founded by Mary Baker Eddy. Rejects orthodox medical practice, in particular blood transfusions or organ donation.

Chupacabra - from chupar "to suck" and cabra "goat", literally "goat sucker"), is a legendary cryptid (a creature whose existence has been suggested but is regarded as highly unlikely) rumored to inhabit parts of the Americas. It is associated more recently with sightings of an allegedly unknown animal in Puerto Rico (where these sightings were first reported), Mexico, and the United States, especially in the latter's Latin American communities. The name comes from the animal's reported habit of attacking and drinking the blood of livestock, especially goats. Physical descriptions of the creature vary. Eyewitness sightings have been claimed as early as 1990 in Puerto Rico, and have since been reported as far north as Maine, and as far south as Chile. It is supposedly a heavy creature, the size of a small bear, with a row of spines reaching from the neck to the base of the tail. Biologists and wildlife management officials view the chupacabra as a contemporary legend.

Circle- Sitting In - A group of people who hold séances, they meet, sit in a circle and meditate before trying to bring forth spirit. A popular practice amongst spiritualists.

Circumambulism - Ceremonial walking around an object or person to secure protection.

Clairaudience - An auditory form of ESP paranormal information is received outside the range of normal perception through voices, whispers and auditory impressions.

Clairaudience - Hearing voices, astral music or discarnate beings.

Clairoleofactor - To have an extraordinary sense of smell, as if you could smell flowers before they bloom or smell trouble before it occurs or death before it happens.

Clairsentience - The ability to clearly feel yours and/or another's emotions and sensations.

Clairvoyance - To have lucid mental perceptions and keen insights about people and life situations and to have clear visual mental images, pictures, to "see" auras and other psychic phenomena. Classic Haunting - (also called an 'intelligent haunting' or 'traditional haunting') Rare, a sentient spirit that can manifest itself into an apparition and communicate with the living; the ghost responds to outside stimuli like questions and statements; it can be friendly or hostile and will let you know the difference; they are sometimes capable of opening and closing doors and windows and moving objects like furniture around.

Clairvoyant - A person with the unexplained ability of knowing about people, things, places or events before they appear or happen. Future sight or knowledge.

Clairvoyant Medium - Or clairvoyant. A person who obtains information paranormally (often by spirit communication) without the need to enter into a trance state.

Cleansing - An informal act used to rid a person(s) or place of unwanted energies.

Climacterics - The belief that certain years in a person's life are more significant in terms of fortune and change.

Closed Deck - A set of cards used in a card guessing deck in which each card will appear a fixed number of times. The statistical analysis obtained from a closed card deck differs from that of an open card deck.

Cloud dissolving - The practice of making clouds disappear at will. Sometimes used as an easy illusion, as small fair-weather clouds tend to dissolve naturally within twenty minutes of forming.

Cluricaune - In Irish folklore, a leprechaun.

Cockatrice - A mythical creature with bird wings, a dragon's tail and a cock's head. Said to be able to kill with a glance.

Cocytus - Classical name of one of the five rivers of Hell. The unburied were said to walk beside the rivers for a hundred years.

Coincidence - The occurrence, within a short space of time, of two or more meaningfully related events and without any apparent causal connection or cause between them. Coincidences are sometimes bizarre and extraordinarily improbable but still are no more-than chance events.

Cold Reading - A technique commonly used in sessions such as psychic readings, in which the person conducting the session elicits information from the subject without their awareness, then uses this information to create the illusion of supernatural ability.

Cold Spot - An unexplainable, cold area in an environment with an otherwise warm, stable, and natural temperature. Associated with the belief that paranormal phenomena are drawing energy to manifest themselves in some way.

Collective Apparition - A rare type of sighting in which more than one person sees the same apparition or phenomena.

Collective Unconscious - Concept put forward by C.G. Jung to refer to a level of unconscious thought and experience shared collectively by humans.

Communication - In medium ship, a message purported to be from a discarnate entity.

Communicator - A discarnate entity from whom the medium receives messages. See also drop-in communicator.

Compass - You can use them for navigation, but on a ghost hunting expedition the primary role is as the low tech back up for your EMF gear. A compass reacts to changes in the Earth's magnetic field and since it is your backup do not buy an electronic compass. A glow in the dark needle is nice.

Confabulation - A term used to describe when real-life experiences are mixed with imagined ones.

Confederate - A person who secretly provides information to a fraudulent psychic or mentalist.

Conjuration - The practice of attracting the attention and involvement of spirits by means of ritual activities.

Conjuring - The process of calling preternatural forces into aid or action through the use of sorcery or ceremonial black magic.

Contact Mind Reading - A technique simulating telepathy, in which the perceived mind reader who generally holds a hand responds to slight muscle movements produced unconsciously by the person whose mind is apparently being read. Also known as muscle reading and no paranormal or psychic ability is needed.

Continuance - Commonly referred to as life-after-death, survival of the psyche post cessation of the biological organism which had generated it.

Control - This is a procedure in paranormal psychology that ensures that the experiment is conducted in a standard fashion so that the results will not be influenced by any extraneous factors.

Control Group - A group of outside subjects whose performance or abilities are compared with the experimental subjects.

Correlation - An association between two or more events or variable results.

Correlation Coefficient - A mathematical of the degree of association between two or more measures used for comparison.

Cosmic Consciousness - A blissful experience in which the person becomes aware of the whole universe as a living being. A spiritual of mystical state of being, can be described as an altered state also.

Coulomb - A unit quantity of electric charge (equals the quantity of charge in approximately 6 x 1019 of electrons.

Coven - A group of practicing witches who meet to socialize and share knowledge and experience, practicing magic as a group or individually.

Crop circles - A crop circle is a sizable pattern created by the flattening of a crop such as wheat, barley, rye, or maize. In 1991, self-professed pranksters Doug Bower and Dave Chorley stated that they had started the phenomenon in 1978 by making actual circles on crops with the use of simple tools. However, crop patterns did not only persist but became astonishingly complex. Some even came to resemble stereotypical extraterrestrials as portrayed by science fiction movies, fractals and archaeological, religious or mythological symbols, thus leading to speculation and passionate debate.

Crisis Apparition - An apparition that is seen when a person is seriously ill, seriously injured or at the point of death.

Cross-correspondence - (a) Separate items of information, received independently by two or more mediums, which make sense only when pieced together. (b) The cross-correspondences are a classic case of highly complex cross-correspondences which continued from 1901 to 1932 among a group of automatists associated with the Society for Psychical Research.

Crossroads - The meeting and parting of ways has always been considered magical. In addition, crossroads are said to be haunted by various entities who lead confused travelers astray. It is also said that on All Hollow's Eve (Halloween), spirits of the dead appear at a crossroad.

Cross-Species Communication - To have a special rapport and understanding with animals, plants or alien beings.

Cryptid - Any species of animal which has not been formally identified or categorized by science. Are legendary creatures that are suspected to exist, but no solid proof of this exists in the scientific community.

Cryptesthesia - refers to information gathered by the senses that enters conscious awareness by some other form.

Cryptomnesia - Knowledge (picked up in a non-paranormal way about a person) that may be revealed without the person knowing or remembering its source, being regurgitated parrot fashion back to them. Such memories may falsely appear to be paranormal revelations.

Cryptozoologist - the study of evidence tending to substantiate the existence of, or the search for, creatures whose reported existence is unproved.

Crypto-zoology - "study of hidden animals") refers to the search for animals which are considered to be legendary or otherwise nonexistent by mainstream biology. This includes looking for living examples of animals which are extinct, such as dinosaurs; animals whose existence lacks physical support but which appear in myths, legends, or are reported, such as Bigfoot and Chupacabra and wild animals dramatically outside of their normal geographic ranges, such as phantom cats or "ABCs" (an initials commonly used by cryptozoologists that stands for Alien Big Cats).

Crystal Gazing - Staring into reflecting surfaces such as a mirror, glass, crystals or water in order to obtain paranormal information and incite. The object itself if not terribly important, it just provides a focus for the psychic to enable them to quickly tune in with their innate ability.

Crystallomancy - The art of gazing into a crystal globe, a pool of water, a mirror, or any transparent object. The person may put him/herself into a hypnotic state to see visions or to summon forth spirits or demons.

Crystal Skulls - The crystal skulls are a number of human skull hard stone carvings made from clear or milky quartz rock, known in art history as "rock crystal", claimed to be pre-Columbian Mesoamerican artifacts by their alleged finders. However, none of the specimens made available for scientific study has been authenticated as pre-Columbian in origin. The results of these studies demonstrated that those examined were manufactured in the mid-19th century or later, almost certainly in Europe. Despite some claims presented in an assortment of popularizing literature, legends of crystal skulls with mystical powers do not figure in genuine Mesoamerican or other Native American mythologies and spiritual accounts. The skulls are often claimed to exhibit paranormal phenomena by some members of the New Age movement, and have often been portrayed as such in fiction.

Curse - To invoke preternatural forces to cause harm or injury to a person, place or object.

Cyclomancy - is a form of divination based on spinning an object and deriving predictions or conclusions from the object's final resting direction. In some traditions, a wheel or top is spun on a surface marked with letters or symbols, and those that fall closest to the device's pointer are consulted. In other traditions, any suitable object may be spun and its direction may be used to obtain a simple yes/no answer or directional indicator. For example an object with a distinguishing feature may be spun between two diverging paths or disparate objects, and the one closest to the feature is chosen. The party game Spin the Bottle is loosely based on this concept.

Dactylomancy - Any of a variety of methods of using rings; for example, by using a ring as a pendulum or dropping it into a glass of water.

Daemon - In Greek mythology, a being who part mortal is and part god. May be benevolent or malevolent. The Greek spellings are used in modern times to distinguish Greek daemons from Jewish and Christian demons.

Day of the Dead - A special holiday, each year to honor the dead it involves parties, feasts, special foods, songs and parades. The most elaborate ceremonies for the dead occur in Mexico.

Dead Sea Scrolls - a number of leather, papyrus and copper scrolls collaborating on the books in the Old Testament of the Bible, found in 1948 in caves on the northwest coast of the Dead Sea, believed to have been written between 168 B.C. and A.D. 233.

Death - The physical extinction of a living things life. Many people do not accept or believe that physical death is the end of our spirit or personality.

Deathbed Visions - A dying person has an awareness of the presence of dead relatives or friends, these visitors are said to come and assist the dying with the transition from life to death.

Death chart - A figure in astrology constructed to show the date and/or time of death.

Death panorama - An out-of-body experience for the newly-deceased, in which the person's life is shown to them as a panoramic view. This experience is said to last for two to three days.

Death prayer 1. A prayer said by the living for the dead, to help the deceased in the afterlife or to ask for help for the living.

Death prayer 2. A technique used to cause the death of a person, for example, commanding a demon to murder.

Debunk - Reported paranormal evidence or paranormal activity is said to be "debunked" when a simple, logical and non-paranormal explanation can account for the reported event(s). Even if the activity is genuinely paranormal, if a simple and reasonable explanation can also be applied, because of this ambiguity a prudent paranormal investigator has to side with the debunking explanation until further evidence of paranormal activity can be obtained. Care has to be used since it is easy to be skeptical of any report or evidence. Usually if the non-paranormal explanation is complex or requires many assumptions it may be over analyzing the situation.

Decibel - A unit to measure relative loudness (or the difference in power usually between acoustic or electric signals). The smallest amount of change that can be detected by the human ear is 1 decibel. The decibel scale is not linear; it is exponential.

Deep Trace Medium - A psychic who allows a spirit to enter their body so that the spirits can communicate through them.

Deja-Vu - Certain events and experiences seem as if you are re-experiencing the event or situation that has happened at another time. As familiar as the experiences are, you cannot recall nor figure out when they happened.

Deliverance - To deliver a human from the oppression or possession of a demonic spirit.

Delta - A term used to refer to any kind of anomalous event.

Dematerialization - This word is used to describe a spirit or specter meaning to deprive of or lose apparent physical substance or in simpler terms, without flesh.

Demon - In religion and mythology, occultism and folklore, a demon (or daemon, daimon) is a supernatural being that is generally described as a malevolent spirit; however, the original neutral connotations of the Greek word daimon does not carry the negative ones that were later projected onto it, as Christianity spread. In Ancient Near Eastern religions as well as in the derived Abrahamic traditions, including ancient and medieval Christian demonology, a demon is considered an "unclean spirit" which may cause demonic possession, to be addressed with an act of exorcism. In Western occultism and Renaissance magic, which grew out of an amalgamation of pagan Greco-Roman, Jewish and Christian tradition, a demon is considered a spiritual entity that may be conjured and controlled. Believed to take the form of "demons" in many forms of religion are:

1. Angels in the Christian belief who fell from heaven (grace).

2. Human souls said to be genii or familiars.

3. Deceased family members that have continued existence and/or possess the ability to influence the fortune of the living.

4. Ghosts or other malevolent visible ghost or animated corpse.

Demonic Haunting - A haunting by a nonhuman entity. Can be very dramatic, even violent. Demonic hauntings often start out with subtle and relatively simple paranormal activity, and then quickly increase to stronger activity. Most often affects people or families that are already under great personal stress from conditions such as alcohol or drug use, psychological or emotional problems, family or marital problems, etc. It is believed the nonhuman entity takes advantage of people in such weaken psychological and emotional condition. Persons who believe them and/or their families are the subject of a demonic haunting should immediately seek both professional paranormal assistance and counseling help.

Demonic Possession - Possession by evil spirits. A person may believe that they have been taken over by an evil entity.

Demonic Sins - A description of the seven deadly sins, with the belief that each is controlled by one of seven demons: Lucifer (pride), Mammon (avarice), Asmodeus (lechery), Satan (anger), Beelzebub (gluttony), Leviathan (envy), Belphegor (sloth).

Demonic Spirit - An entity or spirit spawning from the devil that is or was of this earth. They have the capability of human possession, and the strength greater than any flesh and blood creature. Usually demonic spirits are distinguished by their dark, or black masses of psychic energy.

Demonologist - Involved in the study of Demonology.

Demonology - One who studies and practices the art of demonology. An individual who specializes in the removal of evil or demonic forces from a given environment using the art of demonology. One who brings demonic forces out of their slumber to be cast away. Someone who uses the art of demonology to incarnate demons for ones use in battling them.

Demonomancy - The assistance of demons.

Deport - The paranormal nonphysical movement of objects out of a secure enclosed space. The ability to influence the physical world and objects with just your mind power alone.

Devil - An upper level evil spirit working for Lucifer (Beelzebub, among many).

Devil's mark - A birthmark or other blemish on a person, said to have been placed there by the Devil as a sign of ownership.

Devil's Triangle - A synonym for the Bermuda Triangle. Sometimes used to refer to the Dragon's Triangle in the Pacific Ocean.

Diabolical - Pertaining to or caused by a devil.

Dice Test - An experimental test in which a subject attempts to influence the fall of dice. This study is used for the investigation of psychokinesis.

Digital - Using a binary code (ones and zeroes), discrete, non-continuous values, to represent information.

Digital Recorder - A device used to capture and encode audio into a digital format. Non-digital sources are processed using analog-to-digital (ADC) conversion while playback capability utilizes digital-to-analog (DAC) conversion. Basic digital recording interprets changes in air pressure, chroma and luminance values through time into a stream of numbers. These numbers represent the signal received and decoded into digital format. The most difficult technological hurdle involves simultaneously receiving signal data while coding these signals into digital bits of information. Recording two channels of audio at 44.1 kHz requires the digital recording software to handle 1,411,200 bps (bits per second). The number of bits representing any specific sound wave, otherwise known as the word size, affects signal distortion. If the word size is greater than 24 bits, it more than likely will overload the analog circuitry. Digital recorders cannot process anything higher than this current maximum, in regards to the signal-to-noise ratio. Additionally, if the sample rate is too low or high, the output will be corrupted. Digital recorders are a great investigative tool and usually lend the most credible form of evidence in the form of EVP.

Dimensional Discontinuity - A parallel universe out-of-phase with the one we live in. When this universe aligns with ours, gateways may form which could be portals for spirits.

Direct Voice Phenomenon (DVP) - An auditory "spirit" voice that is spoken directly to the sitters at a seance.

Direct Writing - Direct writing is when spirits actually write using any means. This can be done by slate writing or by pen and paper.

Discarnate - Existing outside a physical body. Having no physical body or form.

Discernment - The ability to feel or perceive something with the use the mind and the senses. A charism or spiritual gift that supernaturally enables a Christian believer to distinguish between holy and unholy spirits through the power of the Holy Spirit. This gift is thought to be especially necessary in instances when individuals may need to be delivered or healed of Demonic possession.

Disembodied - A spirit functioning without a body.

Disembodied Voice - A voice that is heard that comes from no physical body, also known as EVP.

Displacement - Responses on a psi test that correspond systematically to targets other than the intended one for example, a psychic giving you the wrong answer to the current question, but that answer proving to be correct for the next question.

Dissociation - Activity performed outside of normal conscious awareness, or mental processes that suggest the existence of separate centers of consciousness.

Divination - The supernatural art of prophesy; foretelling the future. Examples of divinatory practices are geomancy, tarot, and reading the tea leaves.

Diviner – A person who uses special powers to predict future events.

Divining Rod - A forked rod from a tree said to indicate the presence of water or minerals underground.

DMILS - Abbreviation of Direct Mental Interaction with Living Systems. Used to denote instances where one person is attempting to influence a distant biological system, usually the physiology of another person. As it is unclear whether this represents an influence (see psychokinesis), a case of ESP on the part of the influence (see ESP) or an opportunistic selection process, the term 'interaction' has been adopted.

Dogman - Is a cryptozoological creature first reported in 1887 in Wexford County, Michigan. Sightings have been reported in several locations throughout Michigan, primarily in the northwestern quadrant of the Lower Peninsula. In 1987, the legend of the Michigan Dogman gained popularity when a disc jockey at WTCM-FM recorded a song about the creature and its reported sightings.

Doppelganger - In fiction, folklore, and popular culture, a doppelganger is a ghostly double of a living person, often perceived as a sinister form of bilocation. In the vernacular, the word doppelganger has come to refer to any double or look-alike of a person. The word is also used to describe the sensation of having glimpsed oneself in peripheral vision, in a position where there is no chance that it could have been a reflection. They are generally regarded as harbingers of bad luck. In some traditions, a doppelgänger seen by a person's friends or relatives portends illness or danger, while seeing one's own doppelganger is an omen of death. In Norse mythology, a vardoger is a ghostly double who precedes a living person and is seen performing their actions in advance.

Double - A duplicate of one's own body.

Double Blind - An experimental procedure in which neither the subject nor experimenter is aware of key features of the experiment.

Down Through Technique (DT) - An experimental test for clairvoyance in which the person guesses the order of a stacked series of target symbols (e.g., cards) from top to bottom.

Dowsing - A technique which employs a forked stick, bent wire or pendulum to locate things. To be able to find underground water and/or underground minerals.

Dracula - The name of a vampire in the Bram Stoker novel of the same name (published 1897).

Dragon - A mythical creature generally represented (in western society) as a huge, winged, sometimes fire-breathing reptile with crested head, a long tail, and enormous claws and teeth.

Dragon's Triangle - One of 12 Vile Vortices originally plotted by Ivan T. Sanderson.

Dream Communication - A method by which recently passed spirits may communicate with their surviving loved ones. Through such dreams, spirits relay their goodbyes, important messages, or other concerns.

Drop-in Communication - An uninvited communicator or spirit who 'drops in' at a séance or may even invade and temporarily take over a mediums body in order to communicate in physical form.

Dust/Powders - A specific control object used to document impressions. These substances cover a specific area, in order to capture physical prints from an unknown source. They can also inform/confirm an investigator if the perimeter of a closed off area has been breached, and contamination of the site.

Dwarf - A nature spirit that is short, dark, ranging in height from two inches to two feet.

Dybbuk - A Jewish ghost that takes possession of people.

Earthbound - A spirit being trapped on or remaining on the earthly plane.

Earthquake effect - A paranormal event in which a room shakes as if in an earthquake.

Earth Lights - Luminous phenomena typically shaped in ball form or irregular patches of light appearing randomly and defying explanation. Balls of light that appear to issue directly from the earth, and often appear repeatedly in specific locations. The term was coined by Paul Devereux in 1982; but prior to that they were known as spook lights

EBE - Extraterrestrial Biological Entity.

Eblis - Alternate spelling of Iblis, the renamed demon Azazel was ejected from Heaven.

Ebu Gogo - Three feet tall, hairy little people with pot bellies and long arms sighted on the island of Flores, Indonesia. Tiny females are said to have long, pendulous breasts.

Echolalia - A professional clinical word that means to repeat back what you hear. As applied to the paranormal field it means when a ghost or spirit repeats back something you have just said in order to show they are there and are trying to communicate with you.

ECM - Environmental Communication Mode.

Ecstasy - An altered state of consciousness in which the person experiences great rapture, joy and peace.

Ectoplasm - A product of psychic energy which usually forms as a fog like mist, solid white mass, or vortexes. A white filmy substance pouring from a medium's bodily openings, supposedly denoting the presence of a disembodied spirit.

EEG, Electro-encephalography - A method of recording variations of electrical activity in the cortex of the brain.

E Field Pod - The E-field Pod is to assist a Paranormal Investigator make an informed decision based on Electro-Static evidence collected during an investigation. When you are performing your investigation, team members will often refer to the hair standing up on their arms or the back of their neck. The E-Field Pod can help to detect this invisible E-field that causes this condition. Static electricity is the buildup of electrical charges on the surface of some object or material. Static Electricity can consist of extremely high voltage; this device can sense those high-voltage electrically charged objects at a great distance at detection sensitivity as low as 500mV.

Electromagnetic Energy - A hybrid of electrical charges and magnetic fields that binds nature together.

Electronic Voice Phenomena EVP - EVP's are the recorded disembodied voices of what is believed to be spirits. These voices are often not heard while recording is being performed but are heard when the recording is played back. Related to Instrumental Trans communication.

Electrokinesis - The act of generating electricity using only the mind.

Elemental Spirit - A lesser spirit associated to the fundamentals of nature (fire, earth, wind and water).

Elixir - A liquid or powder said to provide eternal life or life enhancement.

Elongation - A phenomena in which a psychic's body is seen to grow longer under the influence of a spirit.

Electromagnetic Field Flashlight - Whenever operating in a near total dark environment, it is a good idea to bring mobile light sources with you. Flashlights can help your team coordinate and sometimes find your way out of a confusing or overwhelming situation. They can also induce paranormal activity in rare cases.

EMF - Electromagnetic Field (EMF) meters measure levels of electromagnetic radiation - which ghost hunters believe apparitions emit when they are attempting to manifest. This radiation originates from a wide variety of sources, including the earth, people, electronics and power lines. Quality Paranormal Investigators will use an EMF Detector to do baseline readings prior to the investigation and debunk anything showing up before the investigation and log it.

Empath-Empathy - Someone who shows considerable empathy, especially on a psychic level as they are able to tune in and accurately describe the exact emotions or emotional state people were in at the time of the event being investigated. The ability to understand the experience or emotional state of another person or animal. Often used to refer to an apparently psychic ability to experience another person's sensations, pain or emotions. Having psychic empathy has been regarded as a mixed blessing, as the empath must learn to gain a measure of control over this ability.

Energy Lights - These show up on photos as colored lights during some manifestations of hauntings. They usually are not visible to the naked eye and can appear in different colors such as red, orange or green.

Entity - A disembodied or preternatural spirit. A human, animal, or nonhuman spirit.

Epicenter - A focal point or origin of activity. Used in relation to poltergeist phenomena where a single person, unconsciously projecting strong negative energies, may be creating the poltergeist activity through psycho kinesis.

ESP Extrasensory Perception - Perceptions coming from other than the normal senses and originating by supernatural means.

Etheric body - A non-physical body of vital forces or energy, said to accompany a person's physical body.

Evil eye - In witchcraft and black magic, the ability to cast spells and excerpt power over people merely by looking at them.

Evil Spell - Words spoken or written in order to influence others magically, causing them harm and misfortune.

Evocations - are special spells that use a variety of different tools to invoke a physical appearance or manifestation of an angel. Some of these tools might include: incense, candles, books, knives and circles drawn upon the floor. However the component(s) may vary according to the type of spell being used. Incense is one of the more frequently used tools as there is a belief that

the ethereal smoke is required as a substance in which the angel may make
itself seen.

EVP - Electronic Voice Phenomena - EVP's are the recorded disembodied
voices of what is believed to be spirits. These voices are often not heard while
recording is being performed but are heard when the recording is played back.
Related to Instrumental Trans communication.

Exopolitics - Political institutions and processes associated with extraterrestrial
life.

Exorcism - The banishment of an entity or entities i.e. spirits, ghosts and
demons that is thought to possess or haunt a location or human being or
animal. The ritual, which can be religious in nature, is conducted by an exorcist
who will call upon a Higher Power to cast away any evil forces that may reside
there.

Exorcist - One who conducts the rites of exorcism.

Experiment - A test carried out under controlled conditions.

Experimental Group - A group of subjects who undergo a specific experimental
procedure. Often results from this group are compared with those of a control
group.

Experimenter - The person who conducts the experiment and is responsible
for it.

Experimenter Effect - Influence that the experimenter's personality or
behavior may have on the results of an experiment. It is vitally important that
the person in charge of an experiment remains unemotional about the
outcome and as impartial as possible.

Extradimensional - Originating outside our normal space-time reality possibly
from a previously unknown dimension.

Extra-terrestrials - Defined as life that does not originate from Earth. It is unknown whether any such life exists or ever existed in the past, although many scientists think it likely that on Mars, for instance, life either exists or has existed. Extrasensory Perception ESP - Perceptions coming from other than the normal senses and originating by supernatural means.

Fairy - An elemental spirit considered benign but inclined to mischief.

Faith Healing - To expect that one will get better is one of the necessary factors in every type of cure, this confidence that one will be cured comes from a desire to live.

Fakir - An Indian holy man who lives by begging and is said to possess magical powers.

Fallen Angels - Discarnate entities who live close to earth and are desirous and capable of haunting earthlings.

False Anomalies - Any unexplained phenomena captured by instrumentation or film that appears to be a true paranormal manifestation but which, in fact, can be readily explained by natural, environmental conditions.

False Awakening - The event in which a person believes they are awake but are actually dreaming.

Familiar - A live cat or other animal owned by a witch upon which she transfers psychic energy in cases of evil-oriented activities.

Fan Death - The belief that sleeping in a closed room with a running electric fan can cause death.

Faraday Cage - A wire mesh enclosure or cage that provides a shield to radio waves and electrical current.

Fascinate - The act of casting a spell or throwing the evil eye on a person.

Fear Cage - A term used to describe a confined area such as a walk in closet, hallway or basement with very high EMF readings. The combination of being close and confined within an area of strong EMF often brings out extremely great feelings of uneasiness, anxiety, paranoia and/or uncontrollable fear. When this occurs the best thing is to quickly and calmly leave the area and go to a more open area with lower EMF.

Feng Shui - Chinese study of hidden forces and currents thought to be present in the earthly environment.

Fetish - An object used to represent and create a bond with the spirit world. Common fetish objects include dolls, stones, animal teeth and claws.

Findhorn - A spiritual community founded in 1962, in northern Scotland. The community garden was said to produce superior crops due to supernatural assistance.

Fire Walking - Walking on red-hot coals, without pain or damage to the feet. It is accomplished by mind over matter.

Flying Rods - A phenomena in which mysterious rod-shaped objects appear in video footage or photographs.

Flying Saucer - A term, coined in 1947, to refer to unknown disk-like aerial objects, often believed to be extraterrestrial spacecraft. The term has now been largely superseded by 'UFO' Unidentified flying objects.

Focal Person - Person who appears to be at the center of poltergeist activity.

Forer Effects - The tendency of people to interpret statements about personality traits as being accurate for them personally, even when they are not.

Fortean Phenomena - An umbrella term to describe any paranormal phenomena. Named after researcher Charles Fort (1874-1932) who spent much of his life cataloguing such phenomena.

Fortune Telling - Various and different practices which aim to divine future events.

Frankincense - A gum resin of trees of the Boswellia family used to invoke the etheric world helpers for guidance and protection.

Frank's Box - A controversial tool within the paranormal field. Developed by a man named Frank Sumption, this box is also known as the "Telephone to the Dead," a device that can allegedly communicate with the other side. Frank's Box scans AM and FM frequencies in a continuous fashion, thus creating white noise, which in theory spirits can use to interact as questions are asked of them and reply as if you are talking. Frank Sumption made the box using radio, electric and computer components. He made the first box in 2002, after being "prompted to do so from the spirit world". At the time, he made less than 3 dozen, and eventually gave a few of them out to selective participants so that they could test them out for themselves to see if the boxes could be used to communicate with spirits from the other side. There are many variations of his original design.

Free-Response Testing - An ESP or PSI test in which the subject responds freely and does not choose from a fixed list of targets. For example, the subject may write down or draw their impressions, or may talk freely into a tape recorder. In order to assess the accuracy of the responses, they are compared the actual target and are then rated for accuracy judge.

Frequency - The rate per second of a vibration constituting a wave, e.g. sound, light, or radio waves.

Gamalei - Natural stones or gems that are said to be under strong astrological influence. In medieval times they were believed to assist magical powers.

Ganzfeld stimulation - A parapsychology technique developed in the 1970s to provide a low-stimulus environment, in order to improve ESP receptivity.

Gauss - Unit of magnetic induction in the electromagnetic and Gaussian systems of units, equal to 1 maxwell per square centimeter or 10-4 weber per square meter (also known as abtesla).

Gaussia System - A combination of the electrostatic and electromagnetic systems of units (esu and emu), in which electrostatic quantities are expressed in esu and magnetic and electromagnetic quantities in emu, with appropriate use of the conversion constant c (the speed of light) between the two systems. Also known as Gaussian units.

Gaussmeter - A magnetometer whose scale is graduated in gauss or kilogauss, and usually measures only the intensity, and not the direction, of the magnetic field.

Geller effect - The ability to bend metal by paranormal means; named after famed Israeli paranormalist Uri Geller.

Ganzfeild - A state of mild sensory deprivation, characterized by the presentation of homogenous sensory fields. Thus, a person in Ganzfeld will have diffusive plastic hemispheres over their eyes while in a dimly red-lit room, be listening to white noise through headphones, and be seated in a comfortable, semi-reclined chair. Its use in parapsychology is based on a noise-reduction model.

Gematric - A Kabbalistic system of uncovering hidden meaning in text by using letters and numbers.

Genii - In the Gnostic hierarchy, the rank of Angels. In Arabic lore, the jinx.

Geomancy - Any type of divination involving the interpretation of lines or figures.

Ghost - A generic term referring to a form of apparition or supernatural entity. According to traditional belief, a ghost is the soul or spirit of a deceased person, taken to be capable of appearing in visible form or otherwise manifesting itself to the living. Descriptions of the apparition of ghosts vary widely: the mode of manifestation can range from an invisible presence to translucent or wispy shapes, to realistic, life-like visions.

Ghost Box - A device used for contacting spirits through the use of radio frequency. These devices or so called Ghost box also known as Spirit box or Frank's box are used as an electronic medium for the purpose of direct communication with a spirit.

Ghostbuster - A person who removes a ghost, poltergeist, spirit entity, or spectral activity from a haunted site.

Ghost Hunter - Someone who investigates ghostly unexplained activity.

Ghost Investigation - A carefully controlled research project in which various methods and equipment are used to investigate reports of paranormal activity.

Ghost Lights - Floating spectral lights resembling flames or balls, also known as spook lights, earth lights and will-o'-the-wisps, are luminous balls of light seen moving about in nature. Primarily seen outdoors, sightings of ghost lights have been reported all over our world (United States, Mexico, Norway, and Australia, for example) and are likely caused, many cases, by natural, explainable occurrences.

Ghost Seers - The belief that people born at a certain time of day or on certain days possess the clairvoyant power to see ghosts and things that other people cannot see.

Ghost Ship - The appearance of a ship that has been known to have wrecked or disappeared years or centuries before to fore warn of a pending disaster.

Ghost Vehicle - A land vehicles that suddenly appears than suddenly disappears in the blink of an eye. Ghost cars and ghost trains are often seen and heard speeding past before evaporating into thin air.

Ghoul - Demonic or parasitic entity that feeds upon human remains.

Geiger Counters - Used to detect changes in background radiation; measures radioactive intensity in MR/hr. (milli-Roentgens per hour).

Giant Anaconda - Reports have been made of 100 feet long snakes on the Rio Negro of the Amazon River basin.

Giant Octopus - The Blue Holes of Bimini, offer many sightings of these unknown huge, many-tentacle animals.

Giant Sloth - Weighing up to 3 tons, these supposedly extinct animals have been reported in South America in contemporary times.

Glastonbury - A sacred site in England, said to be one of the oldest in Britain.

Glastonbury Scripts - A series of manuscripts written between 1907 and 1912 using automatic writing. The scripts were produced under the guidance of architect Frederick Bligh and relate to the restoration of Glastonbury Abbey.

Glastonbury zodiac - A 15km-wide circular earth zodiac in England, centered on Butleigh with Glastonbury Tor at the northwest.

Globsters - Strange looking giant creatures (also called blobs) wash up on the beaches of the world, get the media and scientists excited, and sometimes turn out to be "unknowns".

Globule - (Known as orbs) a small sphere of electromagnetic energy, in which the spirit usually appears on film as globules.

Glossolalia - Speech which is apparently meaningless gibberish, but which some interpret as meaningful or divine, for example, the Christian practice of "speaking in tongues".

Goat - An experiment in which the subject does not believe in the ability for which they are being tested.

Goblin - A nature spirit showing itself as small, swarthy, and malicious, capable of shape-shifting to become an animal, thief, or villain, name given to the more mischievous and grotesque-looking fairies.

Gnomes - Nature spirits made of pure elemental substance, living underground, in mines, and in rocks.

Gnosticism - Derived from the Greek word gnosis, meaning knowledge. A religious movement in the Mediterranean between the first century BC and third century AD.

Goetic - Relating to a kind of magic concerned with evoking evil spirits and compelling them to serve humans.

Grateful Dead - Ghosts of the dead return to the living to reward deserving people.

Gray Lady - A female ghost who awaits the appearance or return of her long lost lover.

Gremlin - A small, pesky spirit, generally friendly in nature, given to mischief and pranks involving electrical and mechanical equipment. Gremlins appear to be particularly fond of aircraft, and they were first acknowledged by the British Royal Air Force in World War I after pilots on dangerous missions reported seeing misty, goblin like spirits in their aircraft.

Grigori (Watchers) - A collective term for fallen angels. It was said that Grigori were sent to guide and assist man during the beginning of civilization.

Guardian Angel - These are Angels who are assigned to protect all living creatures. Each person is said to have their own Guardian Angel.

Guardian Spirit - A personal protective spirit often thought to be an angel.

Guide - A spirit who is believed to assist a person's spiritual journey or impart accurate information to psychics to impart to those who seek their services for a psychic reading.

Half Real Objective - When you perceive nothing subjectively but obtain objective documentation.

Half Real Subjective - When you subjectively perceive something that was not documented via objective means.

Halloween - "All Hallows Eve", the night of October 31st, when the worlds of spirits and mortals are said to become one.

Hallucination - The perception of sights and sounds that are not actually present.

Harbinger - A person or thing that announces or signals the approach of something.

Haunt - A ghost that returns to the same location is said to haunt it. Ghosts generally haunt places, not people, however it is not unusual for a spirit to attach itself to a particular individual or family due to a familial connection.

Haunted - A person, place or an object to which a spirit is attached. The spirits can be human or inhuman in nature.

Haunted Location - An area that is believed to be occupied by paranormal activity.

Haunting - Paranormal phenomena such as apparitions, unexplained sounds, smells or other sensations that are associated over a period of time within a specific location or surrounding a certain person. It can be caused by an intelligent Entity or Residual Energy.

Healer - Someone who is thought to somehow have the ability to heal.

Healing - The cessation of illness or disease not bought about by medicine or conventional treatments. Generally indicates cures that cannot be explained in terms of accepted medical practice.

Hecate - In Greek mythology, a demon goddess of witchcraft, darkness and death.

Hellhound / Black Shuck - A spectral death omen in the form of a ghostly dog.

Herbalist - A practitioner who understands plants for their medicinal use knows where they grow, how to prepare them for healing various kinds of diseases, and how to use them in everyday life.

Hermetica - A school of mystical thought that, together with the Kabbalah, formed the original foundation of Western occultism.

Hertz - Electromagnetic field frequency generated by an alternating current (or the number of waves (or cycles) per second).

Hex - To use BLACK MAGIC to harm another person's body, family or property by means of deep concentration. A magical spell, usually with malevolent purposes such as a curse. The term is derived from the German word Hexe for a witch.

Hexagram - Two interlaced equilateral triangles, one apex pointing up and one apex pointing down.

Hinduism- Ageless religion of India.

Hoax - Anything deliberately faked or being passed off as legitimate paranormal phenomena for the purpose of notoriety, money, or other personal gain.

Hobgoblin - A term typically applied in folktales to describe a friendly but troublesome creature of the Seelie court. The most commonly known Hobgoblin is the character Puck in Shakespeare's A Midsummer Night's Dream. Puck, however, is only another name given to a much older character named Robin Goodfellow. However, the origins of his name can be controversial. Hobgoblins seem to be small, hairy little men who—like their close relative, Brownies—are often found within human dwellings, doing odd jobs around the house while the family is lost in sleep. Such chores are typically small deeds, like dusting and ironing. Oftentimes, the only compensation necessary in return for these was food. Attempts to give them clothing would often banish them forever, though whether they take offense to such gifts or are simply too proud to work in new clothes differs from teller to teller.

Holy Grail - The holy cup used in Jesus Christ's last supper.

Holy Water - Water that has been blessed by a member of the clergy. Holy water is said to have the ability negate negative forces.

Homeopathy - A natural medical discipline that combines natural ingredients, typically in immeasurably small doses, to promote health and healing.

Honey Island Swamp Monster - Reportedly these "Swamp Thing" monsters are seen in the Louisiana swamps.

Hope Diamond - A cursed jewel supposedly torn from the brow of a temple God. The diamond has brought tragedy to those who have owned it.

Horary astrology - A form of astrology in which a question is answered by using a chart based on the time the question is proposed.

Horoscope - A foundation concept in astrology that involves interpreting the character and destiny of a person based on celestial positions at the time of birth.

Hot Reading - A devious or fraudulent reading in which the reader has been given prior knowledge of the sitter.

Hot Spot - Any area where a higher than average temperature inconsistent with the environs is recorded along with paranormal phenomena. Could also refer to a very active haunted locale.

House Blessing - A minor exorcism of a home performed by a priest.

Human Sacrifice - The ceremonial killing of a person as an offering to an evil spirit for magical purposes.

Human Spirit - The (earthbound) spirit of a deceased person.

Humidity Meter -This is a meter that gauges the amount of water vapor in a given parcel of air. Humidity is represented as absolute and specific. Absolute humidity is the quantity of water that exists in a particular parcel of air, measured in cubic meters. Relative humidity is measured as the ratio of partial water vapor pressure to the saturated vapor pressure at a specific air temperature. The dew point is the temperature at which water vapor saturates a given parcel of air. Simply put, the dew point equals one hundred percent humidity. Measuring the moisture content in ambient air will allow investigators to attributive photographic or video evidence to water vapor, mist or fog. Conversely, the higher the humidity, the higher energy potential for a given parcel of air. This can hypothetically influence our visualization of physical manifestations.

Huna - A Hawaiian religious observance involving clairvoyance, precognition, healing, miracles and ritual.

Hyperaesthesia - Exceptionally acute sensory acuity.

Hypercube - A higher dimensional object that's impossible for our three dimensional minds to visualize.

Hypnagogic State - A relaxed state occurring while or just at the point of dropping off to sleep.

Hypnopompic Imagery - Imagery occurring in the hypnopompic state occurring at the point where you regain awareness after sleep.

Hypnosis - Represents the alpha and theta levels of consciousness that one also reaches during sleep. The subject acts only on external suggestion.

Iblis - The primary devil in the Koran.

I Ching - Ancient Chinese 'Book of Changes'. Consisting of 64 hexagrams patterns of 6 broken and unbroken lines which are used in a divinatory practice involving the throwing of yarrow stalks or three coins to answer one's psychological, business, or social problem.

Ignis fatuus - A phosphorescent or spectral light that that is alleged to be an indication of death. This phenomenon is thought to be caused by spontaneous combustion of gases emitted by rotting organic matter.

Illuminism - The process of attaining spiritual enlightenment.

Illusion - A delusional perception between what is perceived and what is reality.

Immortality - The belief in immortal beings and stories about them can be found in many faiths and cultures.

Immortal - A living or un-dead soul who cannot die or be destroyed.

Imp - A nature spirit who does more harm than good to the earthling.

Imprint - It is theorized that events and strong feelings/emotions can leave a copy or record of themselves on places (tunnels, rooms, fields etc.) and objects (furniture, buildings, personal affects etc.). Most notably this occurs when a sudden and violent death occurs such as a powerful accident, a murder or other crime, a war or battle area etc. The energy that is left can result in a non-intelligent haunting, usually a residual haunting. In these cases people often report seeing and hearing the same thing over and over like a tape playing, rewinding and playing again. Sometimes the event seems to be recorded on the specific location rather than a building, room or object. There have been cases reported where an imprint haunting has occurred in a building, the building is later totally demolished and a new one built (or the area just left vacant) but the haunting still continues. In the situation of imprinting on an object the haunting can follow the object through several owners. This is often reported with items purchased at a yard sale or flea market.

Incantation - is a charm or spell created using words. An incantation may take place during a ritual, either a hymn or prayer, and may invoke or praise a deity. In magic, occultism, and witchcraft it is used with the intention of casting a spell on an object or a person.

Incarnate - Living in a physical body.

Incarnation - literally means embodied in flesh or taking on flesh. It refers to the conception and birth of a sentient creature that is the material manifestation of an entity, god or force whose original nature is immaterial. In its religious context the word is used to mean the descent from Heaven of a god, or divine being in human/animal form on Earth.

Incorporeal - means without a physical body, presence or form. It is often used in reference to souls, spirits, the Christian God or the Divine.

Incorruptibility - Inexplicable lack of decay in an aged corpse. Various cultures have both chosen to view this as a sign of an evil doer or saint.

Incubus - A demon in male form supposed to lie upon sleepers, especially women, in order to have sexual intercourse with them, according to a number of mythological and legendary traditions. Its female counterpart is the succubus. An incubus may pursue sexual relations with a woman in order to father a child, as in the legend of Merlin. Religious tradition holds that repeated intercourse with an incubus or succubus may result in the deterioration of health, or even death. Medieval legend claims that demons, both male and female, sexually prey on human beings. They generally prey upon the victim while he or she is sleeping.

Indirect Voice - Mediumistic phenomenon in which the discarnate entity appears to speak using the vocal apparatus of the medium.

Infestation - Repeated and persistent paranormal phenomena.

Infrared - A part of the electromagnetic spectrum that is below visible range. IR cameras allow one to see in the dark and pick up on activity that the physical eye cannot.

Infrared Imaging/Thermal - Thermography, or the science of infrared imaging, detects radiation in the infrared range of the electromagnetic spectrum (900-14,000 nanometers). The black body radiation law dictates that one can see an environment without the need of visible illumination because objects body temperatures emit radiation. Warm surfaces stand contrast well against cooler backgrounds. Used primarily in the military, security, engineering and fire-protection; thermal imaging is utilized to find people or a localized heat source. A thermographic camera use a CMOS focal plane array (FPA) instead of CCD sensors. Common formats of FPA technology: InSb, InGaAs, HgCdTe and QWIP. Newest technology employs un-cooled micro bolometers FPA sensors. Two forms of thermography, passive and active. Passive shows features of interest stand out prominently against a cooler ambient background. Active displays more of a thermal contrast between differing surfaces temperatures. The ability to visualize temperature fluctuations remains a valuable tool for paranormal investigators.

Infrasonic - Pitches too low to be heard by humans. Though we can't hear infra sound vibrations, we can often feel them, because parts of the body resonate in this range.

Inhuman spirit - An entity or spirit of a being that has never lived in the earthly realm. These spirits are inhuman and have never been a human. They exist as an entity of their own. Some claim that inhuman spirits are demons or evil spirits that were cast out of heaven with Satan. These spirits roam the earth in search of someone whom they can possess.

Inner Voice - Receiving guidance and assistance from inside of you, intuitive thoughts or feelings. People with various beliefs will attribute the "messages" to different sources such as God, angels, The Universe, Spirit, etc.

Intelligent Haunting - An intelligent haunting is thought by some to be a haunting by a responsive entity, and dynamic in nature unlike a residual haunting. A characteristic of an intelligent haunting is the ability of the phenomenon imposed by the entity to have free will or to make conscious decisions.

Interpolation - A method used to increase the resolution of an image by adding pixels to an image based on the value of surrounding pixels.

Intuition - Act of knowing without the use of usual rational processes. Based partly on subconscious pattern association of known information, and partly on subconscious psi impressions.

Investigation - An organized group of researchers in search of paranormal phenomena to document with scientific instrumentation.

Invocations - are very similar to evocations, however there is one main difference; i.e., the person trying to summon the angel tries to persuade it to enter their body as opposed to physically appearing. This is so they can communicate. Although far more dangerous it is considered an easier thing to do.

Ion - An electrical charged atom or molecule.

Ion Counters - Used to count the number of free-floating ions in the air; measures ion density in units of ions per cubic centimeter (ions/cm2).

Ionization - The removal of electrons from an atom so that it becomes charged.

IOvilus - The iOvilus produces speech based on changes to sensors in the iPhone or iPod Touch. Simply, the idea is that an outside force can affect a change that registers a response.   Instrumental Trans Communications "ITC" Device is used by the investigator to communicate with a spirit by asking questions or telling it to interact.

IR (Infrared) - Infrared light is light from the lower end (long wave length/low frequency) of the electromagnetic spectrum (between the visible light spectrum and microwaves). IR light is not visible to the naked human eye without the use of special equipment. IR is not to be confused with thermal imaging. While IR and thermal energy are both on the short end of the electromagnetic spectrum they are not the same thing. There is evidence that ghosts/spirits and other paranormal entities may be more susceptible to being viewed (including video and image photography) using the IR light spectrum. IR sensors are also often used for measuring temperature and detecting movement.

IR Camera - Allows one to take a photo in the dark and picks up on activity that the physical eye cannot.

Jamais vu - A feeling that a familiar place or situation has never been experienced before. The opposite of Deja-Vu.

Jersey Devil - a legendary creature or cryptid said to inhabit the Pine Barrens in southern New Jersey. The creature is often described as a flying biped with hooves, but there are many variations.

Joule - Unit of electrical energy (equal to the work done when a current of 1 ampere is produced by a potential of 1 volt across its terminals.

Joy Touch - A meditative technique developed by Pete A. Sander Jr. which is said to help treat various conditions including obesity, depression, paranoia and others.

Judaism - A religion which holds the belief that every human being has a right to justice, purity, and truth which even the power of kings cannot erase.

K2 Meter - A K2 meter picks up on the energy fields that spirits disturb when they are present in the environment.

Ka - Ancient Egyptian term for the double or astral body.

Kabbalah - Jewish mystical tradition based on Old Testament revelation.

Kap Dwa - A 12-foot tall two-headed giant, allegedly captured by Spanish sailors in 1673.

Karma - A widely held belief that 'as you sows, so shall you reap. No good deed will go unrewarded and no bad one unpunished. The theory of inevitable consequence. "What goes around comes around".

Kia - A trancelike state of emotional ECSTASY wherein the SHAMAN has enhanced awareness.

Kinetic Energy - Description for the movement of objects by a ghost. A physical manifestation of an unseen force which may move, throw or even destroy objects. These ghosts are known as "Poltergeists" (German for "noisy ghost").

Kirlian Photography - A method created by a Russian named Seymon Kirlian where a paper is placed on top of a grounded metal plate, a picture is taken with a high frequency electric current and when developed you're able to see the "aura" of the object.

Kobald - A German malicious spirit who haunted metal-bearing mines.

Kongamato - The natives of the Jiundu region of Northern Rhodesia (now Zambia) have firsthand encounters with these strange flying bat-like creatures.

Kundalini - The energy of human consciousness which is normally dormant, lying near the root chakra at the base of the spine. "Serpent Power", is often represented in drawings as two coiled serpents much like the Caduceus.

Lake Champlain Monster - Commonly known as "Champ", a legendary monster said to inhabit Lake Champlain.

Lake Storsjon Monster - Lake Seljord in the Telemark region of Norway has its own Lake Monsters swimming the waters here for centuries.

Lau - Are certain African lakes the home to 40 feet long unknown catfishes or lungfishes.

Legion - The term used to describe the multitude and myriad of evil spirits.

Lemures - A ghost who returns to haunt its living relatives. This spirit was so named by ancient Romans.

Lemuria - Legendary lost continent of the Indian Ocean, rumoured to be the original Garden of Eden.

Leprechaun - In Irish mythology, an elf-like creature around 1 meter tall.

Levitation - The process by which an object is suspended by a physical force against gravity, in a stable position without solid physical contact.

Ley Lines - The theoretical lines that can be drawn to connect ancient (and some modern) sites across a country, even around the world. The term "Ley Line" ("Ley" being a Saxon word meaning meadow or cleared strip of ground) was first coined by Alfred Watkins in the early 1920's. He noticed that many ancient and prehistoric structures (e.g. mounds, stone circles, temples, river crossings, ceremonial hilltops, etc.) could be connected by straight lines. Often these lines exactly fit compass directions, and sometimes at certain times of the year match up with star alignments. He also noticed that many of these lines intersect and where they intersect are significant other structures such as churches, temples, and burial grounds. Some people believe Ley Lines also follow the natural magnetic forces of the Earth and therefore are very powerful for spiritual and mystic activity. Ley lines are also known as corpse ways, church paths, church lines, and coffin lines.

Life Review - A flashback of a person's life that is typically associated with near-death experiences.

Light Rod - A light rod appears as a bar or stick like shape. When a light rod sometimes takes a bend, it is then called a swirling light rod.

"Lights Out" Investigation - A paranormal investigation, usually conducted indoors and at night, where all the light sources and other electronic devices in the building have been turned off. The equipment used for paranormal investigations is typically more sensitive at night and in the dark. Having lights off reduces the possibility of false or misleading evidence caused by reflections and glares.

Light Trance Medium - A person whom spirits can communicate through without going into a deep trance state.

Lilith - Is believed to have originated as a female Mesopotamian storm demon associated with wind and was thought to be a bearer of disease, illness, and death.

Limbo - A level of consciousness which comprises one of the seven planes in the density in the etheric world.

Living Ghost - The manifestation of a ghost or entity, usually a living close family member or friend, which appears a long distance (sometimes hundreds or even thousands of miles away!). This event usually coincides when the other person (the one manifesting) is facing an immediate great stress or life-threatening danger. Examples include an aircraft pilot or crew flying through a storm, a soldier on the battle field, an automobile driver or passenger during a sever accident, etc. Some believe this is related to astral projection and out-of-the-body experiences. This phenomenon is related to the moment of mortality manifestation.

Loch Ness Monster - Nessie is the most famous Lake Monster in the world; they are said to inhabit this loch, an extremely deep Scottish lake.

Lore - All the facts and traditions about a particular subject that have been accumulated over time through education or experience.

Lost Time - With paranormal ghost/spirit activity it is possible that a small concentrated area of high paranormal activity may briefly alter the physical environment such that time slows down or stops altogether. For example, a person in such an effected area may be in the area for 20 minutes as measured by a clock outside the area. But the person's watch only shows them in the area for 15 minutes. What happened to the 5 minutes difference? This phenomenon is similar to what sometimes in reported UFO cases.

Low Magic - To use amulets, talismans, handed down rituals, chants and incantations as an aid to help the magician perform his or her psychic feats.

Lucid dreams - The ability to control what happens in your dreams. Often associated with feelings of aliveness and freedom.

Lucifer - Satan, leader of the rebellious angels.

Luminous Phenomena - A frequent occurrence in physical medium ship. On rare occasions such phenomena have been witnessed in apparent independence of mediumistic conditions. The experience of strange lights or glows, often around objects or people. These lights seem to have been the result of an outpouring of the combined psychic forces that religious ecstasy supposedly generates.

Lycanthropy - In folklore, the ability of a person to change into animal form. In psychiatry, the delusion of having been transformed into an animal.

Lying on of Hands - a form of healing practice that involves the healer placing his or her hands near the body of a sick person.

Macro-PK - Psychokinetic effects that can be directly observed rather than only inferred from statistical analysis.

MacFarlane's Bear - The carcass is at the Smithsonian, believed to be a possible hybrid between a grizzly and polar bear or a new unknown species.

Magic - Sometimes known as sorcery, is the practice of consciousness manipulation and/or autosuggestion to achieve a desired result, usually by techniques described in various conceptual systems. The practice is often influenced by ideas of religion, mysticism, and occultism.

Magic Circle - An imaginary circle drawn with a pointed finger or magical item or a real circle made with substance.

Magic Square - A square array of numbers in which the sum of each row, column and diagonal is the same. In some ancient cultures, thought to have magical powers.

Magician - A person who practices some form of magic. In popular culture a magician is an entertainer, although this type of magician is more properly referred to as an illusionist.

Magnetometer EMF - An instrument for measuring the magnitude and direction of a magnetic field typically used by paranormal researchers to detect a ghost's magnetic energy.

Magnetosphere - Magnetic field surrounding the earth.

Mahatma - A master of esoteric knowledge, a guru.

Maleficia - "Evil happenings", misfortunes and catastrophes with no obvious earthly cause, attributed to the influence of witchcraft, evil spirits, etc.

Malevolent - A spirit that wishes to do harm.

Malicious - Spirits that destroy or damage things of a personal or financial value for the sake of hurting others.

Mammon - Demon mentioned in the New Testament (Matthew, 6,4). Has come to be known as the demon of money, or the demon of love of money.

Mandala - In Buddhism and Hinduism, a symbolic diagram of the universe used for ritual purposes.

Manifest/Manifestation - The act of an entity trying to make itself appear in our world. Entities are believed to exist mainly as energy with no physical form. When an entity is trying to make itself appear or make its presence known in our world it is said to be manifesting itself; trying to make itself into some form of physical state.

Mantra - A sacred sound, string of words or sacred syllables used to facilitate deeper meditation.

Mapinguari - A prehistoric cryptid that reportedly lived in the Amazon rain forests of South America.

Marian Apparitions - The event in which the Virgin Mary is seen.

Match - Another or alternative term for hit when referring to a correct piece of information given by a psychic.

Matching Tests - Card guessing tests in which the subject uses key cards when making guesses. See also blind matching, open matching, and screen touch matching. Virtually useless for testing psychic ability or responses in my opinion.

Materialization - The act of forming something solid from the air. One of the most difficult and impressive materializations is when part or all of a ghost or spirit can be seen, especially if the face is recognizable.

Matrixing - The natural propensity of the human mind to rationalize sensory input to make more sense. Example: As children, we "see pictures" in the clouds.

Maxwell (Mx) - The basic unit of magnetic flux in the CGS system, equal to the flux through one square centimeter perpendicular to a magnetic field with an intensity on one gauss; one maxwell equals 10 weber.

Meditation - A disciplined mind technique for a set time to achieve a high state of consciousness.

Medium - Someone who professes to be able communicate with spirits on behalf of another living being, acting as a midway point halfway between the worlds of the living and the dead.

Mediumship - What a Medium does or is. Activity of a medium.

Men in Black - A phenomena associated with UFO sightings, in which men dressed in black appear. It is claimed that these men assist in cover-ups and discourage witnesses from speaking publicly. This phenomena was made famous in the "Men in Black" movies.

Mentalism - A branch of conjuring or magic involving the simulation of psi.

Mesmerism - A hypnotic induction of a sleep or trance state. A system of healing, involving the induction of trance states and the supposed transfer of animal magnetism.

Metal Bending - Psychokinetic ability to bend metal objects.

Metamorphosis - Shape-shifting. Changing and shifting either or your physical or mental self into another form or object such as an animal or tree.

Metaphysics - Derived from the Latin word Meta which means beyond, metaphysics would literally mean that which is beyond the laws of physics.

Metempsychosis - An alternative term for reincarnation.

Miracle - An unexpected event attributed to divine intervention. Sometimes an event is also attributed to a miracle worker, saint, or religious leader. A miracle is sometimes thought of as a perceptible interruption of the laws of nature. Others suggest that God may work with the laws of nature to perform what people perceive as miracles. Theologians say that, with divine providence, God regularly works through created nature yet is free to work without, above, or against it as well. A miracle is often considered a fortuitous event: compare with an Act of God.

Micro-PK - Psychokinetic effects that cannot be directly observed, but only inferred from the statistical analysis or manipulation of data.

Milligauss (MG) - 1/1000 of a gauss.

Milliwatts per square meter (mW/m2) - A unit for measuring one joule of work per second of power per square meter.

Mist - A Photographed anomaly that appears as a blanket of light. There is no substantial proof that these are related to paranormal phenomenon.

Mngwa - The Mngwa are cats described as being as large as donkeys, with marks like a tabby and living in Africa - but not a known species.

Mokele-mbembe - A lake monster said to inhabit the swamps in the Republic of the Congo and central Africa.

Moment of Mortality - A ghostly manifestation that occurs when someone is at the exact moment of their death. A ghost, spirit or other apparition appears to a close friend or family member. Can happen over great distances (hundreds, even thousands, of miles away). This phenomenon is similar to the living ghost and Death Bed Visions phenomena.

Mongolian Death Worm - Locals in the Gobi Desert of Mongolia talk of these giant snakes, worms, or long thin lizards (also called Olgoi-khorkhoi or Allghoi-khorkhoi) as killing livestock and people with their breath.

Moon - A natural satellite of a planet. "The Moon" is the official name of Earth's only natural satellite. The Moon is a common and powerful force in many systems of belief and folklore.

Mothman - A creature reportedly sighted numerous times in Point Pleasant, West Virginia, USA, between November 1966 and November 1967. Mothman was said to be a man-sized creature with wings and large reflective or luminous eyes.

Motion Detectors - A device used that contains a physical, electronic or infrared sensor array that quantifies motion into a triggered response. Electronic motion transcribes motion into an electrical signal. Often, optical or acoustical changes are measured within the detector's field of view is required. Dual technology motion detectors can have a series of sensor arrays, measuring numerous forms of motion and produce a myriad of tiered responses. Passive infrared sensors look for heat fluctuations that cross the beam. Active ultrasonic sensors bounce pulses of low-frequency sound and measure the reflection off a passing object. Active microwave sensors send out microwave pulses and measure the reflection off the nearby object, similar to a police radar gun. These devices are great tools for both preventing intrusion into an uncontaminated site and to verify roaming EMF or temperature fluctuations.

Motor Automatism - Bodily movement or functions that are accompanied but not controlled by consciousness.

Mx (Maxwell) - The basic unit of magnetic flux in the CGS system, equal to the flux through one square centimeter perpendicular to a magnetic field with an intensity on one gauss; one maxwell equals 10 weber.

Mystery Helicopters - Unmarked helicopters, often colored black, which have been reported flying near the scenes of unusual paranormal activity (e.g. cattle mutilations, UFO sightings).

Mystic - One who brings new knowledge of spiritual truths (proven or not) incorporates psychic skills and psychic healings with religion.

Mystical Experience - Involving experiences of ecstasy, unity, timelessness, loss of self, divine revelation, or spirit communication.

Mysticism - Religious or spiritual doctrines which argue that the human mind or soul can directly experience and feel the divine.

Mythology - The accumulated collection of myths, folklore, legends and ancient stories from a given culture.

Nandi Bear - A cryptid named for the Nandi people among whom it was reported to have lived in western Kenya.

Natural - A rare phenomena that appears ghostly but in fact is created by some scientifically unknown property of the present nature.

Natural Light - Other mobile light sources include candles, torches, matches, etc. It is extremely unlikely and unwise to use natural light in place of flashlights for safety concerns. You don't want to accidentally drop a candle onto a homeowner's carpet, burning their place to the ground! It's best to just use natural light in a controlled environment and/or for inducing paranormal activity.

Nature spirits - Spirits said to exist in nature, usually invisible to mortals. May be good or evil.

Nazca Lines - A series of ancient geoglyphs located in the Nazca Desert of Peru. They have been designated a UNESCO World Heritage Site. The high, arid plateau stretches more than 80 kilometres (50 mi) between the towns of Nazca and Palpa on the Pampas de Jumana. Although some local geoglyphs resemble Paracas motifs, scholars believe the Nazca Lines were created by the Nazca culture between 200 BCE and 700 CE. The hundreds of individual figures range in complexity from simple lines to stylized hummingbirds, spiders, monkeys, fish, sharks or orcas, llamas, and lizards.

Near Death Experience (NDE) - An experience that is reported by people who clinically die, or come close to actual death and are revived. These events often include encounters with spirit guides, seeing dead relatives or friends, life review, out-of-body Experiences (OBE), or a moment of decision where they are able to decide or are told to turn back.

Necromancy - The attempt to conjure, summon or raise the dead in order to learn secrets and insights from the spirits. Usually intended to gain personal advantage or fortune over others. The person who is trying to perform the necromancy process is called a Necromancer. This deals heavily into the unsavory realm of magic, spells, and dark/forbidden witchcraft rituals. Can also be attempted with Tarot cards and Ouija boards. Regardless of the process used, necromancy is highly dangerous from the point of view that you are opening a doorway and have no idea what thing may come through and into your life! Necronomicon - The book of the dead.

New Age - A broad term used to describe a range of beliefs and ideas, often including mysticism, astrology, parapsychology, etc.

Newton - Unit of force required to accelerate a mass of one kilogram one meter per second.

Nexus - The transitional, or joining point connecting physical matter (which, in a sense, is energy condensed) and pure energy, and containing properties of both definites, i.e. the physical brain producing a mind through its network of dendrites and firing axioms', or the body's connection to the spirit. The concept of the Nexus is the basis for much conjecture and postulating.

Night Shot - A setting common on hand held video cameras. Originally it was a term used to describe the night vision (total darkness) recording capability of the Sony Handicam series of camcorders. This term has since become synonymous with meaning any night vision/total darkness video camera or recording device regardless of the manufacturer. The night shot feature uses a built-in IR (infra-red) illumination source. An external IR illuminator can often be attached for additional viewing range.

Night Vision - A part of the electromagnetic spectrum that is below visible range. This technology is made possible through two techniques: sufficient spectral and sufficient intensity range. Spectral range methods help the viewer become more sensitive to light. Enhancing the spectral range allows the observer to visualize near-infrared or ultraviolet radiation. Intensity range dictates that the human visual system can potentially perceive single photons under the most ideal of conditions; however, due to neurological and environmental noise, we are limited to a few tens of photons. Animals have better night-vision than humans due to a larger eyeball, lens, optical aperture, more retinal rods, and tapetum lucidum and improved neurological filtering developed through evolution and biology. Intensity range finders utilize image intensifiers, a gain multiplication CCD, or other low-noise, high-sensitivity array of photo detectors. Night-vision is useful like thermal imaging because it allows field investigators to perceive their environment more completely while operating in near total darkness.

Night Vision Devices (NVD) - Use image-enhancement technology to magnify available light to see in low-light conditions.

Nocturnal Lights - One of the six Hynek categories of Unidentified Flying Objects UFO's, defined as unexplained lights seen in the night sky.

Null hypothesis - The hypothesis that experimental results are due to chance.

Numerology - The study of numbers in regard to a person's character and life plan.

NVD (Night Vision Devices) - Use image-enhancement technology to magnify available light to see in low-light conditions.

Occam's Razor - The principle that we should always prefer and look for the simplest explanation of events.

Occult - From the Latin, meaning something that is concealed or covered. Since the 16th century, it has meant anything that is mysterious. Today in America, it generally refers to magical, mystical and experimental studies.

Occultism - Knowledge of the hidden and mysterious forces.

Ogopogo - This is Canada's most famous type of water monsters, inhabitants of Lake Okanagan in the south central interior of British Columbia.

Ohm - A unit of electrical resistance (equal to that of a conductor in which a current of 1 ampere is produced by a potential of 1 volt across its terminals.

Ohmmeter - An instrument for measurement in ohms of the resistance of a conductor.

Old Hag Syndrome - A nocturnal phenomena that involves a feeling of immobilization, suffocation, odd smells and feelings and is sometimes accompanied my immense fear.

Old Soul - One who has been incarnated innumerable times.

Olfactory - Of or relating to the sense of smell.

Omen - An event interpreted as a prediction of a future event.

Oppression - The first stage of a haunting where the invading demonic entity attempts to gain access to the location or person targeted for victimization. The demonic spirit begins working on the persons mind, interjecting thoughts of negative behaviors and actions.

Optics - used to capture visual evidence. We use high quality digital cameras with a vast array of accessories to cover a wide spectrum including laser grids. We have cameras that allow us to record video in complete darkness. We also have heat sensing capabilities which allow us to record non-visible heat anomalies.

Oracle - Any person or thing that serves as an agent of divine communication. Oracles were thought to be portals through which the gods spoke directly to people. In this sense they were different from seers who interpreted signs sent by the gods through bird signs, animal entrails, and other various methods.

Orang-Pendak - These reportedly small biped small apes (also called Sedapa) live in the jungles of Sumatra and Borneo.

Orbaphilia - A chronic condition suffered by unscrupulous unintelligent and or mentally disturbed amateur ghost hunters; technically defined as someone who loves photographically obtained or video captured orbs regardless of how they came to be and claim nevertheless that they are in fact paranormal; a thorn in the side of serious researchers everywhere.

Orbs - Orbs appear to be a form of energy of an unknown origin. An orb can take different shapes. They can also be seen by the naked eye, but most of the time you only get orb sightings in photographs, and on video tape (VHS). They seem to defy gravity and change directions quickly. They seem to also twinkle. The presences of people make them react. They appear both indoors and outdoors. False orbs tend to be transparent and pale white, or blue. Real genuine orbs tend to appear dense or brighter on film. To increase the probablllty of you getting a photograph of a genuine orb, it is good to take the photograph at the same time as other unusual phenomenon are experienced, such as sharp changes in temperature, and increases in electromagnetic energy. In a genuine orb there is a nucleus. It has concentric circles or bands within. It can be active in visible realm, but more active in infrared. They appear abundantly in supposed haunted locations. Drops of rain, specks of dust, insects, reflections, as well as many other things can be mistaken for orbs.

Orgone Energy - A term used to refer to a universal life force, associated with sexuality.

Original Momentum - The initial force of energy necessary to create motion telekinetically.

Oscilloscopes - Measure and display frequency in wave patterns on a screen.

Ouija board - A board consisting of the letters of the alphabet, numbers 1-0, and words "yes", "no" and "goodbye" which is used as a tool for communicating with spirits. Game board manufactured by the Parker Brothers Company. Used to communicate with what people believe are spirits. Ouija boards, instead, open a pathway for foul spirits and demons to enter. When used by someone with no knowledge of how the board works, or the curious and inexperienced, this can cause problems.

Out Of Body Experience - State in which the spirit of a person travels to the astral plane. It is said that people can in some instances travel to other locations on the physical plane. Also known as OBE, astral projection or remote viewing. Paranormal- Beyond the normal of human or scientific explanation.

Outward Manifestation - The physical manifestation of paranormal activity.

Pagan - One who practices Paganism. A worshiper of a polytheistic religion, although some sects of Christianity consider all non-Christians to be pagan.

Paganism - Is a religion of nature, in other words Pagans revere Nature. Pagans see the divine as immanent in the whole of life and the universe; in every tree, plant, animal and object, man and woman and in the dark side of life as much as in the light. Pagans live their lives attuned to the cycles of Nature, the seasons, life and death.

Palmistry - Encompasses all phases of analyzing one's hands to tune into one's past and future.

Paranormal - Referring to something that is beyond the range of normal human experience or scientific explanation. Paranormal phenomena are distinct from certain hypothetical entities, such as dark matter and dark energy, insofar as paranormal phenomena are inconsistent with the world as already understood through empirical observation coupled with scientific methodology.

Paranormal Investigator - A person that visits locations that are believed to have paranormal activity. They act as an impartial professional that attempts to find out what is causing the activity whether it's paranormal in nature or not. Some 'Hauntings' can be easily debunked as loose pipes, passing cars, poor electrical connections giving the resident peace of mind.

Paranormal Photography - The endeavor of collecting physical evidence of the paranormal in the form of photographs.

Paranormal Research - The study of phenomena that is unexplainable by main stream science.

Para physical - The human body's physical reaction to being exposed to paranormal phenomena. This includes phenomena felt as cold spots, hot spots, electric tingles, goose bumps, hair raising sensations, nausea, vertigo, headaches, etc.

Parapsychologist - One who studies parapsychology; however, this title is not officially recognized in the Unites States, and it is illegal to call one's self a parapsychologist unless they have a degree in psychology from a recognized university.

Parapsychology - The scientific study of phenomena that natural laws cannot explain. Derived from the Latin word para, which means beyond, parapsychology literally means beyond psychology. It is generally defined as the scientific study of paranormal phenomena. Literally beyond psychology. The study of apparent new means of communication, or interaction, between organisms and their environment (commonly referred to as psi, or psychic ability), beyond those presently understood by the scientific community.

Pareidolia - A type of illusion involving seeing defined or distinct objects in non-defined subjects (also called Simulacrd).

Passing Bell - A bell rung in church when a person is near death, in order to frighten away evil spirits who might try to take the departing soul.

Passive Infrared (PIR) - A technique used for IR (infrared) devices that detect infrared without emitting it.

Past Life Recall - remembering or having mental flashes about living in another century.

Past-Life Regression - A technique of hypnosis involving regressing people to alleged previous lives and times.

Pendulum - One of the oldest known types of divination, the pendulum consists of a weight at the end of a flexible cord, chain, etc. When held at one end, the weight will move in a variety of patterns in response to questions from the user.

Pentacle - A 5 pointed star with the single point UP encompassed by a circle. The five points represent the elements (Earth, Air, Fire, Water, and Spirit) and the circle signifies unity. The Pentacle is used for protecting by Wiccans or people who perform Witch Craft. This is not an evil or satanic symbol. It simply signifies the spiritual beliefs of the wearer very similar in comparison to the Christian Cross.

Pentagram - The magical diagram consisting of a five pointed star which is a representation of man, considered by occultists to be the most potent means of conjuring spirits. Pentagrams were used symbolically in ancient Greece and Babylonia, and are used today as a symbol of faith by many Wiccans, akin to the use of the cross by Christians and the Star of David by Jews. The pentagram has magical associations, and many people who practice Neopagan faiths wear jewelry incorporating the symbol. Christians once more commonly used the pentagram to represent the five wounds of Jesus, and it also has associations within Freemasonry.

Percipient - A person who sees (i.e., perceives) an apparition.

Peruvian Mystery Jaguar - Unknown large cats with white background covered in solid irregular spots are seen in the rainforests of Peru.

Phantom - An apparition or specter. Existing only as an energy form.

Phantomania - An occurrence in which the victim is held paralyzed while being subjected to preternatural attack.

Phantom Traveler - A human or animal spirit that haunts a particular road or highway. Often this is a hitchhiker who rides with living people, then inexplicably disappears.

Phenomenology - An approach to research that aims to describe and clarify a person's own experience and understanding of an event or phenomenon.

Phenomenon - A term used to collectively describe anything that cannot be explained in scientific terms.

Photon - The fundamental particle/quantum of electromagnetic radiation (radiant energy); light; has no electrical charge.

Phrenology - The reading of character and mental ability from the shape of a person's skull. A popular practice with the Victorians.

Physical Mediumship - The production of paranormal physical phenomena eg. lights, sounds, materialization, elongation, levitation, by a medium. Physical mediumship often involves a state of trance. See also mental mediumship.

Picture Drawing - A free-response ESP test in which the subject attempts to draw impressions of the target EG. person or object.

Pilot Study - A preliminary study, generally of modest scale.

PIR (Passive Infrared) - A technique used for IR (infrared) devices that detect infrared without emitting it.

Pitch - The highness or lowness of a sound. It is measured by the frequency of its waves in hertz.

Pixels - The individual dots used to display an image on a computer monitor or sensor.

Placebo - An inactive/dummy treatment often given to a control group.

Place Memories - Refers to a location that captures energy and uses it to record an image of an event that once happened there and later replays it. Akin to a residual haunting.

Placement Test - A test for PK in which the subject attempts to influence the place in which dice or other objects land.

Planchette - The indicator or pointer used in association with a Ouija board.

Plasma - Is defined by bluish-white light caused by the ionization of the surrounding area. The ionization process releases photons from the bond of atoms causing a visible glow. Plasma may be created when an invisible electromagnetic force or high energy field moves invisibly through an air mass. In physics and chemistry, plasma is typically an ionized gas. Plasma is considered to be a distinct state of matter, apart from gases, because of its unique properties. "Ionized" refers to presence of one or more free electrons, which is not bound to an atom or molecule. The free electric charges make the plasma electrically conductive so that it responds strongly to electromagnetic fields. Plasmas are the most common phase of matter. Some estimates suggest that up to 99% of matter in the entire visible universe is plasma.

Pocomania - A Jamaican spirit religion, similar to Voodoo.

Poltergeist - a non-human spirit entity which literally means "noisy ghost" but is usually more malicious and destructive than ghosts of dead human beings.

Traditional poltergeists activities are thumping and banging, levitating or the moving of objects, stone throwing and starting fires.

Poltergeist Agent - Phenomena usually surrounding a young child, usually a girl; the (the child) is almost always around when the poltergeist activity occurs; this usually involves objects being thrown around when there is no one around, unexplainable tapping and scratching noises and objects disappearing and reappearing hours, days or weeks later; in worst-case scenarios there can be injuries to human beings from thrown objects and scratches appearing on the flesh of the PA; Fires are also known to occur in the worst cases - sometimes with catastrophic results.

Portal - A multi-dimensional gateway which spirits of the dead may enter or exit from their world into ours. This may be accomplished via a vortex.

Possession - The state in which a living person is controlled by a foreign, malignant entity.

Postmortem Apparition - Apparition that appears more than 12 hours after a person's death.

Post-Mortem Communication - A message delivered to a living person from a deceased one, usually delivered via a medium.

Powders/Dust - A specific control object used to document impressions. These substances cover a specific area, in order to capture physical prints from an unknown source. They can also inform/confirm an investigator if the perimeter of a closed off area has been breached, and contamination of the site.

Prayer - A solemn attempt to communicate with a spiritual being or power.

Precognition - Also called future sight, refers to perception that involves the acquisition of future information that cannot be deduced from presently available and normally acquired sense-based information. The related terms, premonition and presentiment refer to information about future events that is perceived as emotions. The terms are usually used to denote a seemingly parapsychological or extrasensory process of perception, including clairvoyance. Various psychological processes, making no reference to psi, have also been offered to explain the phenomena.

Precognitive Dreams - To have dreams of events or incidents before they happen.

Prediction - A statement from a psychic that claims to foretell future events.

Preexistence - Belief that the personality or soul exists prior to actual birth.

Premonition - A vision or warning of future events.

Presence - Any spirit energy on the earthbound plain. A subjective feeling that a person, animal or discarnate entity is present.

Presentiment - Information about future events which is said to be perceived as emotions. A sense that something unpleasant is about to happen, a feeling of evil to come accompanied by feeling of apprehension and foreboding.

Preternatural - Associated with inhuman, demonic or diabolical spirits or forces.

Pricking - A method of identifying witches during the witch hunts of the 16th and 17th centuries, in which the suspect was jabbed with a sharp object. If they showed no pain they were considered to be a witch.

Primary Readings - Initial measurement of energy taken at a haunted location.

Prophecy - A vision or revelation of the future.

Prophet - A human spokesman for an etheric world to spread a divine message.

Provocation - An effort to provoke or command a spirit to reveal itself.

Pseudoscience - Any type of research or conclusion that has the initial appearance of science, but fails to meet the criteria for scientific validity.

PSI - A general term for parapsychological phenomena that includes informational (RV, ESP) and energetic (PK) effects. Psi, or Y, is the 23rd letter of the Greek alphabet.

Psionic - The use of physical tools to assist in accessing or interpreting ones ESP's.

PSI Phenomenon - Any event which results from, or is an instance of, PSI.

Psyche - Generally refers to the mind.

Psychedelic - Expanding and revealing mind. A class of plants and drugs such as peyote, psilocybin, LSD that can produce such feelings of this effect.

Psychic - Dealing with the ability to see, hear, feel and sense beyond the average human ability. A person with abilities of extrasensory perception or metal telepathy.

Psychic Ability - The ability to sense that outside what is considered normal.

Psychic Attack - The transference of negative energy into a person to deliberately harm.

Psychic Cold - The cold sensation received when a spirit is present, usually having defined boundaries.

Psychic Echo - When sounds from the past have mysteriously recorded themselves into the natural environment.

Psychic Healing - Forms of healing using psychic energy. Eg. lying on of hands and psychic surgery.

Psychic Imprint - Believed by some to be a replayed psychic event which is "recorded" in space and time and continues to loop the same scene over and over again in a particular location. This view portrays the repeating events of a residual haunting as mindless, soulless imprints of past lives, not as the active, intelligent movements of spirit energies.

Psychic Photography - Supernatural or preternatural Images appearing on a photograph.

Psychic Protection - Any deliberate metaphysical method by which a person attempts to ward of spirits.

Psychic Research - The study of psychic phenomena.

Psychic Surgery - The supposed ability to paranormally perform invasive surgery using no conventional medical tools. The psychic surgeon uses either an unsterilized knife, or his bare hands, to appear to make an incision and remove some internal matter. Once the operation is finished, there is no sign of an incision, nor are there any unpleasant aftereffects (e.g. infection). Many of the investigated cases have turned out to be fraudulent, involving sleight of hand tricks to make the operation appear convincing. However, it is possible that, in some circumstances, the ritual nature of the "surgery" could help effect a cure through the equally mysterious placebo effect.

Psycho kinesis (PK) - The power of the mind to affect matter without physical contact, especially in inanimate and remote objects by the exercise of psychic powers.

Psychometry - The ability to acquire knowledge of people, places or object by touching an object associated with it.

Puck - It is a device to communicate with spirits. This plugs into the USB port of your computer and uses Environmental Communication Mode "ECM" technology. The Puck has 9 sensors. A and B Voltage, EMF (electromagnetic levels) 1 and 2, and EMF (natural magnetic fields) 1 -4, and a temperature sensor. The Puck does multi-process data gathering, including EMF, Natural EM, and temperature. It has a speech capacity that matches EMF with words in the word bank. Computer will "speak" words based on what is picked up by the recorder and recognized by the program.

Purgatory - In Roman Catholic doctrine, the place where souls of people who have died in grace must suffer while being cleansed of their sins before they can be admitted into heaven.

PX Ovilus Puck - Is a device that interacts with the user and the surrounding environment. This is done by the devices built in sensors that look for emf, temperature and touch.

The PX has seven modes:

1. Dictionary Mode the PX has 2048 internal words that are used in this mode

2. Phonetic Mode the PX will use phonemes to speak

3. Reverse Phonetic Mode The PX will reverse the phonetic output. In effect; it talks backwards

4. Touch Mode this mode is used to detect if the device is being touched

5. Voice Change Mode, this mode is the same as #1 dictionary mode except the voice can be altered detected inputs

6. Repeat Mode say last words said in this mode the PX will repeat the last words spoken from last said to first (up to 400 words).

7. Energy Mode: this mode allows the user to set the sensitivity of the device with preset levels.

The key to using this device is that the investigator needs to interact with it in order to stimulate a response.

Pyramid - A shape which is sometimes said to possess supernatural properties.

Pyrokinesis - The ability to unconsciously control and sometimes in rare cases produce fire with their mind only.

Pyromancy - A form of using fire.

Qabbalah: Alternative spelling of Kabbalah. An esoteric or occult matter resembling the Kabbalah that is traditionally secret.

Quackery - Integrating metaphysics with sympathetic magic or spiritualism with healing. The term is generally used to describe frauds that dispense useless or harmful treatments to vulnerable people on their deathbeds.

Qualitative Method - A research method involving the collection of non-quantitative data (e.g., observations, interviews, subjective reports, case studies).

Quanta - Fundamental units of energy.

Quantitative Method - A research method involving the collection and statistical analysis of numerical data.

Querent - A person who has a session with a medium.

Quintessence 1. In occultism, the fifth element which binds together the other elements (earth, air, fire, water).

Quintessence 2. In alchemy, a synonym for elixir.

Radiation - Energy that is radiated or transmitted in the form of rays, waves or particles.

Radiesthesia - Theory based on the assumption that living organisms emit some kind of radiation or emanation that is capable of being detected using instruments or by dowsing. Similar assumption to the existence of aura or radionics.

Radionics - Use of instruments to detect radiation from living organisms EG radiesthesia.

Radio Voice Phenomenon (RVP) - Receiving the voice of a deceased human being through a regular radio.

Random - Refers to events that are, in principle, haphazard and unpredictable as in by pure chance.

Random Event Generator (REG) - An electronic device which uses a random physical process to generate random events or random numbers.

Random Number Generator (RNG) - Like random event generator.

Rapping's - The knocking sounds apparently produced by spirits in response to questions during a seance.

Raudive Voices - Intelligible voices recorded on magnetic tape under conditions of silence or white noise which is heard only when the tape is played. A phenomenon discovered by Konstantin Raudive.

Reading - Information given by a psychic or medium to a querent.

Real Time - EVP Interactive Digital Voice Recorder - This device allows one to listen to EVP's as they occur live in Real Time, and then interact immediately based on intelligent data gathered during investigations. The device runs parallel microprocessors to encode, decode and extract data from your saved audio file and then play it back to you in a user defined, time selectable window from 1-60 seconds.

Rebirth - In Buddhism, the belief that there is some continuity of mind and spirit from one life to the next. Buddhism, does not accept the existence of the individual soul and therefore does not view rebirth as the soul's literal re-incarnation.

Reciprocal Apparition - An extremely rare type of spirit phenomenon in which both the agent and percipient are able to see and respond to each other.

Recurrent Spontaneous Psychokinesis (RSPK) - A term for poltergeist activity.

Regression - The activation of the subconscious mind to recall parts of the past.

Reiki - A type of healing in which the healer is a channel for universal force and energy.

Reincarnation - The belief that each person possesses a soul which is independent of the body and can be reborn into another body.

Relative humidity - The ratio of the current absolute humidity and that of the highest possible absolute humidity depending on the air temperature.

Relic - An item closely associated with a holy person or saint, usually a part of that person's body or clothing.

Religion - A belief in powers higher than one's self backed by faith rather than logic.

Remote Viewing - The term used when a person is able to "see" a remote object and explain its characteristics and location without ever physically been to the particular location. Used heavily by the US Government, during the height of the Cold War, for spying.

REM Pod - The REM circuit was originally developed to be part of the Mel Meter Series. The REM-Pod uses a mini telescopic antenna to radiate its own independent Magnetic Field around the device. This EM field can be easily influenced by materials and objects that conduct electricity. Based on source proximity, strength and EM field distortion (4) Colorful RED LED lights with sound can be activated in any order or combination.

Repressed Psychokinetic Energy - A theoretical psychic force produced, usually unconsciously, by an individual undergoing physical or mental trauma. When released, some think the power causes paranormal occurrences such as poltergeist activity.

RES - Residual Energy Sighting - Ghost, spirits or entities that repeat its last moment before departing that can be seen.

Residuals - Ghost, spirits or entities that repeat its last moment before departing

Residual Haunting - Experiences from the living that are imprinted in a specific location and are replaying on a cyclical basis, like the playback of a movie, such as apparitions doing the same things or voices and sounds being heard at always the same time of the day. Many hauntings can be of this sort and not necessarily animated by conscious spirits.

Retroactive Psychokinesis - Paranormal influence that an agent can have on an experiment after it has been completed.

Retrocognition - An experience in which a person finds themselves in the past and is able to see and experience events in which they had no prior knowledge.

Revenant - A recently departed spirit who returns very briefly to make contact with loved ones. This may serve as an act of closure before going on to the Afterlife.

Reverse EVP - This device converts your voice into EMF and frequency range. The theory is that a spirit can hear you more easily or better than regular voice.

Ribbon - A ribbon is a seen in videos and pictures as a stream of light and can be a moving orb or the first sign of a vortex forming.

Ritual - A prescribed event or a particular form or ceremony that is built up by tradition, and with it, a great amount of energy.

Ritual Magic - Proven processes and ceremonies used repeatedly .

Runes - Ancient Norse and Germanic alphabet which has been associated with various mystical arts.

Sabbat: The Witches' Sabbath, said to have been a weekly midnight convention attended by warlocks and demons.

Salt - Symbol of the element EARTH because it's a crystalline substance it can receive and hold etheric magnetism better than other substances. Has a property to ward off evil vibrations.

Samhain - One of the "doorways" marking the start of the Celtic year.

Santeria - An African-based religion similar to voodoo, Originating in Cuba and Brazil, which combines the worship of traditional Yoruban religion with the worship of Roman Catholic saints and Native Indian traditions. Slaves imported to the Caribbean to work the sugar plantations practiced and carried on with their religious traditions, including a trance for communicating with their ancestors, animal sacrifice and sacred drumming.

Sasquatch - A legendary creature resembling a large hairy human, said to inhabit the wilderness of the northwestern United States and western Canada.

Satan - God's adversary, expelled from Heaven for rebelling against God.

Satanic - Pertaining to Satan.

Satanism - The Worship of Satan.

Screen Touch Matching - A card-guessing procedure in which the subject and experimenter sit on opposite sides of a screen which has a small gap at the bottom. Key cards are hung on the screen in front of the subject. Underneath each key card is a blank card that can be seen by both subject and experimenter. The experimenter holds the target cards and the subject indicates the guess on each trial by pointing to the corresponding blank card. The experimenter then places the card in a pile on his or her side of the screen in a position corresponding to that of the indicated blank card and all is recorded for later analysis.

Scrying - A term used to cover a wide range of divination techniques which parapsychology would tend to classify as types of ESP. Most scrying techniques involve some degree of fixation on a surface with a clear optical depth (e.g. a crystal ball, a pool of ink or deep water) or on an area which shows random patterns (e.g. flames in a fire, smoke), the idea being that subconscious information available to the scrying will be manifested in their interpretation of the imagery or random patterns they see. Techniques using a clear optical depth are actually very similar to the idea behind the homogenous visual field used in Ganzfeld ESP research.

Seance - A group of dedicated persons and at least one well-grounded medium who sit in a blacked-out room to produce physical phenomena. Groups sit in a circular formation to keep psychic energy concentrated in the center for easier manipulation by the etheric world intelligences.

Second Sight - Celtic folklore concept that would be referred to today as psychic ability, particularly in the realm of divination and precognition.

Sect - A group of people who all believe, or who profess to believe, in the same basic principles of a religious nature.

Seebek Effect - The electrical resistance of a substance that is measured by digital thermometers.

Sensitive - A person who possesses psychic powers. One who can feel the presence of spirit energy through any of the five senses: sight, smell, touch, hearing, and taste.

Sensory Deprivation - Conditions of greatly restricted sensory input. To be deprived of all five senses.

Serpent Power - Kundalini energy.

Shadows - An apparition appearing as a flickering black or smoky gray mass of any size or shape. Often seen out of the corner of the eye before disappearing completely or may be caught on film.

Shaman - Shamanism encompasses the belief that shamans are intermediaries or messengers between the human world and the spirit worlds. Shamans are said to treat ailments/illness by mending the soul. Alleviating traumas affecting the soul/spirit restores the physical body of the individual to balance and wholeness. The shaman also enters supernatural realms or dimensions to obtain solutions to problems afflicting the community. Shamans may visit other worlds/dimensions to bring guidance to misguided souls and to ameliorate illnesses of the human soul caused by foreign elements. The shaman operates primarily within the spiritual world, which in turn affects the human world. The restoration of balance results in the elimination of the ailment.

Shape-Shifting - Ability to assume the form of another person, animal or other entity.

Sheep - An experiment in which the subject believes in the ability in which they are being tested.

Siddhis - Name given to paranormal powers associated with the practice of Yoga.

Sight - Appalachian folklore term referring to psychic ability.

Significance - Results of an experiment are said to be statistically significant when they are very unlikely to be due to chance in a psi test, are more likely to be due to psi. The chance probability is reported as the 'significance level'. To be considered significant, the chance probability must generally be less than 1 in 20 5%, or 0.05.

Simultaneous Dream - A dream whose elements correspond closely with those in the dream of another person. Possibly a shared dream experience.

Simulcra - This is a word used to describe the seeing of faces, figures and images in ordinary, everyday object such as rocks, foliage, etc.

Single-axis meter - A type of EMF (electromagnetic field) detector; can only read magnetic fields toward which the internal coil is pointed.

Sitting - A gathering of individuals, usually led by a medium, for the purpose of receiving spirit manifestations or communication with the dead. Also known as a "séance," a "spirit circle," or simply, a "circle."

Sixth Sense - Popular term for ESP and a term used to describe psychic ability.

Skeptic - A person inclined to discount the reality of the paranormal and to be critical of para psychological research. Generally seeks rational or scientific explanations for the phenomena studied by parapsychologists. May be extremely aggressive in their forceful manner of trying to prove non validity of all psychic subjects.

Skepticism - A philosophical position in which a person seeks answers based on evidence rather than doctrine or pre-conceived beliefs.

Skunk Ape - Also known by the label Myakka "Ape" and other local names (Booger, Swamp Ape), these chimpanzee- or orangutan-like primates have been sighted throughout central and south Florida.

Slate-Writing - Writing that appears on a slate during a seance.

Sleep Paralysis - A state of seeming to be awake but unable to move.

Smudging - To burn a special plant (usually Sage) in an area before a ceremony, a healing, or a lecture, this cleanses the atmosphere of any negativity.

Solar Plexus - Believed to be the Soul of man, the center of the body where one feels the emotions of the universe.

Somnambule - Person who performs physical activity while asleep EG, sleep-walking, a person in a deep hypnotic state.

Soothsayer - Someone who makes predictions about what is going to happen in the future.

Sorcerer - A male who has made a pact with the devil in exchange for magic powers.

Sorceress - A female who has made a pact with the devil in exchange for magic powers.

Sorcery - The practice of Black or White Magic.

Sortilege - Divination by lots.

Soul - The continuing electromagnetic energy field of a human or animal retaining all the characteristics of the once living soul, body, and mind. The soul is thought to weigh 13'5 ounces. As moments after death we become exactly that precise amount lighter.

Soulless Apparition - The image of an inanimate object.

Soul Loss - The loss of vital energy experienced as a result of any kind of physical, emotional, mental, or spiritual trauma.

Soul Rescue - An act of metaphysical intervention between a living person and a spirit whereby the earthbound energy is advised and instructed on how to leave the earthly plain and go into the Light to begin its new afterlife existence. Often a Channeler or psychic will act as the human agent for this event.

Sound - A vibration that travels in waves through almost any medium, including air and water (it cannot travel in a vacuum). It is measured by its pitch, loudness and speed (frequency, wavelength, period, amplitude). Sound travels at 1130 feet per second at 68 degrees Fahrenheit.

Space Beings - Extraterrestrial entities, claimed to be channeled by some mediums.

Space-Time Anomaly - A residual haunting caused by strong emotional feelings embedded within a departed spirit. Negative emotions developed during life become a force holding a spirit earthbound to perform repetitious behavior. This view holds that residual hauntings are caused by active, intelligent spirits consciously repeating their actions while trying to resolve past emotional issues.

Sparkles - A visual effect described as the sparkle of embers falling immediately after a fireworks display. These small, sparkling lights usually occur no closer to the camera than ten feet. They are often 20 to 50 feet away, or more. Sparkles are seen during and especially immediately after the flash on a camera are used. Even the most vivid sparkles will not show up on film. (If they do, check for dust or insects.) Sparkles are paranormal phenomena. "Sparkles" is a proprietary term developed in the 1990s by Fiona Broome during research for Hollow Hill. Other researchers have adopted the term to describe this unique phenomenon.

Spectre - A ghost, entity or apparition (unrecognizable to the viewer).

Spell - A magical command or incantation during which period of time a person or object is held captive by a psychic for the benefit of the psychic.

Spike - A sudden and unexplainable jump on an Electro Magnetic Field Detector (EMF) causing it to quickly rise and fall or "peg" the meter.

Spirit - A collective word, the basic theme is always, "indestructible life". Spirits are believed to exist in an invisible realm that can only be seen under certain circumstances or by people with special abilities.

Spirit Attachment - A type of possession. While the spirit does not actively possess the individual it does become attached to it. Much like haunting a person rather than a place.

Spirit Box - A device used for contacting spirits through the use of radio frequency. These devices or so called Spirit box also known as Ghost Box or Frank's box are used as an electronic medium for the purpose of direct communication with a spirit.

Spirit Cabinet - A spirit cabinet, or simply cabinet, is a solid or curtained enclosure within which the medium sits to allow the spirits to appear unimpeded in darkness. The first spirit cabinet was introduced by the Davenport brothers in the 1850s in New York City. Its use was quickly adopted by many of the leading mediums of the day.

Spirit Communicator - A spirit or ghost that uses a medium in order to communicate with someone either verbally or visually.

Spirit Hypothesis - The theory that individual consciousness survives the death of the physical body in the form of a spirit, and that it may be communicated with, especially through the use of a medium.

Spirit Operator - A spirit or ghost that uses a medium to physically manipulate something on earth.

Spirit Photography - Photographs of figures or faces, believed by some to be those of deceased persons. These photographs are generally hard to prove to be authentic.

Spirit Portal - An area allowing cross traffic between our world and the spirit world. A form of doorway, it sometimes occurs in the form of a vortex.

Spirit Releasement - Contemporary term for an exorcism.

Spirit Theater - A term used by modern-day magicians to describe shows, acts, or tricks in which ghosts or other spirit activity are apparently produced.

Spiritual Guide - A spirit that watches over a living person and that offers wisdom or guidance. Referred to by some as a guardian angel.

Spiritualism - A science, philosophy, and religion using the doctrine of metaphysics, belief in the continuity of life after death and communication with this life for the advancement of civilization and personal growth.

Spiritualist - One who believes in the communication between this world and the invisible world, and who endeavors to mold his or her character and conduct in accordance with the highest teachings derived from such communion.

Spirit World - The place spirits go after death of the human form.

Spontaneous Cases - Paranormal phenomena occurrences that occur in everyday life, unsought, unplanned and unexpected.

Spontaneous Human Combustion (SHC) - A phenomenon where in a living human body allegedly catches fire as the result of intense internal heat.

Spook - A ghost who haunts a particular place. The word's origins are Dutch.

Sprite - A radiant, small nature spirit whose energy blends well with good deeds for earthlings, brings guidance, confidence, honor and security regarding money and opportunities, changes dimensions to be recognized by earthlings.

Star Sign - In astrology, the sign of the zodiac assigned to a person based upon the position of the Sun at the time of their birth.

Static Electricity - An electrical charge that builds up due to friction between two dissimilar materials; friction removes some electrons from one object and then will deposit them on the other.

Steller's Sea Cow - A once thought extinct species, these totally marine animals, looking like huge, wrinkled manatees, and are still being seen by Russian fisherman.

St. Michael - A lofty etheric world Angel who communicated with earthlings during the time of the Old Testament, his function was to be guardian over Israel. In the New Testament, he was the first of the seven Archangels and led the host against the Devil.

Stigmata - Marks on one's body resembling crucifixion wounds, bleeding from these points simulating the wounds of Jesus the Christ.

Subjective Apparitions - Hallucinations of apparitions or other phenomena that are created by our own minds.

Subjective Paranormal Experience (SPE) or Subjective Psi Experience - An experience that the person who has it believes to be paranormal.

Subliminal Perception - Perceiving without conscious awareness. A visual or auditory message that is allegedly perceived psychologically, but not consciously. Perceiving without conscious awareness. Applied to a stimulus below the level of awareness and below the absolute threshold of stimulation, as when an auditory or visual presentation is too weak to have an effect, or at least any effect of which the subject is aware.

Succubus - A female demonic legendary creature who seduces men in their sleep. She often visits monks. Its male counterpart is the incubus. Similar to a vampire, succubi draw energy from men to sustain themselves. In the past succubi were depicted as frightening and demonic, usually with wings and a tail. Sometimes the wings are that of a bat or a bird. The tail takes various shapes, sometimes that of a snake or an aquatic tail like that of a mermaid. In modern times, a succubus may appear in dreams and is often portrayed as a highly attractive seductress or enchantress.

Super-ESP Hypothesis - The suggestion that people are capable of unlimited ESP. The super-ESP hypothesis is often presented as an alternative to the survival hypothesis in explaining mediumistic phenomena a medium is believed to obtain accurate information using super-ESP powers and not directly from the spirit of a deceased person.

Supernatural - Of or relating to existence outside the natural world. As opposed to paranormal, the term "supernatural" often connotes divine or demonic intervention, commonly referred to as to anything outside the bounds of natural laws.

Superstition - The unfounded believe that certain object, activities or rituals can be helpful or harmful.

Survival - The belief that some aspect of the persons, consciousness, mind, personality, soul lives on after death of the body.

Symbolic Apparition - Many apparitions are symbolic and are trying to communicate a message by which they appear to, what times, what they are wearing, what they are doing, etc.

Synchronicity - Meaningful coincidences that often are mediated by subconscious psi activity. Our intuitive/psi faculty nudges our paths into meaningful intersections in times of need.

Table-Tilting - Unexplained movements of a table, usually occurring in a seance when a group of people place their hands on the surface of the table. Often the movements are interpreted as spirit communications. Also known as table-turning or table-tipping. Tables can also be seen to almost hover.

Tactile - Feeling a slight wind in a closed-off room, or a slight tug on a person's clothing with nobody in the immediate vicinity.

Take-away Apparition - The appearance of a deceased person beside a deathbed with the sole purpose of guiding the infirm to the afterlife.

Talisman - Drawings of various shapes and sizes which have specific purposes of good luck.

Tarot Cards - A pack of cards for the purpose of divination using symbolism contains seventy-eight cards. Fifty-Six Major Arcana the rest being minor cards forming a system of communication.

Tasmanian Tiger or Thylacine - Thought extinct, these wolf-like marsupials are still sighted on a regular basis in Western Australia, and perhaps New Guinea too.

Tazelwurm - Classic small log-shaped reptilian cryptids from the European Alps are enigmatic animals, but have they gone extinct in historical times?

Teggie - A legendary creature said to inhabit the Welsh Llyn Tegid (Bala Lake).

Telekinesis - Where objects are remotely displaced and moved around, solely by the powers of the mind.

Telekinetic - A person with the ability to move objects with their mind.

Telepathic - A person who uses telepathy.

Telepathic Projection - A now-discredited theory first espoused by Frederic W.H. Myers, a 19th-century paranormal investigation suggesting that spirits of the dead sent mental messages to the living rather than physically returning as ghosts.

Telepathy - Psychic communication between individuals. The ability to communicate directly through mind-to-mind contact and to perceive information directly from another's mind, without resorting to the use of the traditional five known senses.

Teleportation - A method of transportation in which matter or information is dematerialized, usually instantaneously, at one point and recreated at another.

Telergic - The excitation of the motor or sensory centers take place through the communicating intelligence in some direct way, such as a healing using a pendulum.

Temporal Lobe Activity - Electrical activity in the temporal lobes of the brain. Often associated with strange sensations, time distortions and even hallucinations. Sometimes used as an explanation for seemingly paranormal experiences such as apparitions and alien abduction experiences.

Terrafirm - To be connected with the planet Earth as if it were a part of you.

Thanatology - The study of Near-Death Experiences.

The Light - A portal or entranceway into the afterlife or another dimension and is used by spirits to leave an earthbound existence.

Theosophy - A term applied to a range of mystical philosophies. The word is derived from the Greek Theos (God) and Sophia (wisdom).

Therianthropy - The supposed ability to change from human to animal form and back. As in werewolf type transformations.

Thermal/Infrared Imaging - Thermography, or the science of infrared imaging, detects radiation in the infrared range of the electromagnetic spectrum (900-14,000 nanometers). The black body radiation law dictates that one can see an environment without the need of visible illumination because objects body temperatures emit radiation. Warm surfaces stand contrast well against cooler backgrounds. Used primarily in the military, security, engineering and fire-protection; thermal imaging is utilized to find people or a localized heat source. A thermographic camera use a CMOS focal plane array (FPA) instead of CCD sensors. Common formats of FPA technology: InSb, InGaAs, HgCdTe and QWIP. Newest technology employs un-cooled microbolometers FPA sensors. Two forms of thermography, passive and active. Passive shows features of interest stand out prominently against a cooler ambient background. Active displays more of a thermal contrast between differing surfaces temperatures. The ability to visualize temperature fluctuations remains a valuable tool for paranormal investigators.

Thermometer - This is a device that measures the temperature gradient using several key principles. A thermometer consists of a container/device, a temperature sensor (mercury bulb) and scale/digital readout. Primary thermometers measure matter properties approximately without any unknown quantities. Secondary thermometers are more sensitive than primary but are still calibrated against a primary for fixed temperature readings. The official fixed point temperature scale (International Temperature Scale of 1990) extends from .65 K to 1358 K or -272.5 °C to 1085 °C. Principles of certain substances, namely air, expand and contract as the "temperature" changes. A substance, such as, mercury or water will rise and fall with this air fluctuation, creating a viable scale for measurement. Investigators use thermometers to record ambient air temperature and determine roaming temperature fluctuations.

Theurgy - Magical practices which aim to contact and communicate with the gods.

Third Eye - Associated with the human pineal gland, said to be the mystical center of the body and the focus for meditation.

Thixotropy - This is a property that is exhibited by certain gels. A thrixopic gel maintains its shape and appears solid, but if it is subjected to certain forms of disturbance, such as shaking, it will start to flow like liquid. Possible explanation for bleeding statues etc.

Thoth - Greek name for the Egyptian god of wisdom and magic.

Thought Form - An apparition produced solely by the power of the human mind.

Thoughtography - Paranormal ability to produce images on photographic film by concentrating on a mental image. Most famously demonstrated by Ted Serios images.

Thought Transference - Telepathy

Thunderbird - Large condor-like birds, perhaps Teratorns, roam the skies of North America, along regular migration routes. Time Travel - To project your soul's consciousness out of your body and into a past or future time.

Tone Healing - Your tone of voice affects others by disturbing, catalyzing, esoothing, lulling, inspiring and quite often healing them.

Torah - A sacred book of teachings, an inclusive term that refers to that entire God has revealed about Himself, history of the Jewish people, and the conduct that is required of them.

Touched - The act of experiencing physical contact from a ghost, spirit or other paranormal entity. Can be as simple as a tug on your shirt or pressure on a part of your body to scratches, burns or being pushed/shoved. However, serious physical injury is very rare.

Touch Healing - To impart through your hands soothing and healing vibrations of energy.

Trance - An altered state of consciousness brought about by the willing collaboration between the medium and the etheric world intelligence for the purpose of physical phenomena.

Trance Medium - A person who enters a state of trance in order to produce mediumistic phenomena.

Trance Mediumship - A form of mediumship in which the medium shares his or her energy with a spirit through the use of a trance.

Transchanneling - To have severe personality shifts.

Transmigration of Souls - As in reincarnation.

Transpersonal Psychology - The study of experiences, beliefs and practices that suggest that the sense of self can extend beyond our personal or individual reality.

Transcendence - A temporary, spontaneous experience in which the life force leaves the physical body to bypass the experience of physical pain, the life force hovers close to the physical body.

Transportation Apparitions - The appearance of ghostly cars, ships, motorcycles, carriages, trains, and airplanes. They haunt their old routes.

Triboelectric Series - A list of materials that is sorted according to which materials tend to develop positive charges and which tend to develop negative charges when the materials meet and then separate; materials higher in the series tend to gain a positive charge while those lower on the list tend to gain a negative charge.

TriField Natural EM Meter - The TriField Natural EM Meter was designed to do field measurements for special research. It detects changes in extremely weak static (DC or "natural") electric and magnetic fields, and signals with both a tone and the movement of a needle-type gauge if either the electric or magnetic field changes from previous levels. Its sensitivity is of interest to researchers in the paranormal field. Every type of detectable physical manifestation requires a certain amount of energy. For example, "moving air" requires the expenditure of a small amount of energy to get the air to move initially. A radio and microwave detector is also included, which reads radio power directly. Because man-made AC electric and magnetic fields are very common and could interfere with readings of static fields, the meter has been designed to ignore AC fields.

Trigger Object - A trigger object could be almost anything, use an object which has a reported history of being moved. Such objects could be glassware or old items such as buttons, coins or small picture frame. Any object can be used, however the purpose of using a trigger object is to act as a focus point to measure or record any event, for example movement.

Triple-Axis Meter - A type of EMF meter; uses three coils and three metal plates on an X,Y,Z - axis; that way the user can read fields from three different directions; the metal plates detect AC or DC electric fields; each coil has a different calibration that lets you detect all angles instead of just the area in front of the device; on most models you can switch between each setting or using a computer circuit, reads the sum of the magnetic and electric.

Troll - A nature spirit that inhabits the mountains and has charge of their functions, shows itself as a dwarf or a giant, capable of shape-shifting, can be helpful or capricious and hostile.

True believer syndrome - A term used to describe a person's insistence on believing something that has been unequivocally disproven.

Trumpet - A conical tube used in séances to produce direct voice communication.

Tzuchinoko - Unknown species of snake sighted in the upper elevations of Korea and Japan.

Ucu - The South American Bigfoot live mainly in the Andean foothills.

UFO - Unidentified Flying Object. This term is typically interpreted as "alien spaceship", although technically it simply means what it says — an object flying in the air which has not yet been identified.

Ufology - The study of UFOs.

Ufonaut - An ufonaut (or UFOnaut) is the entity that operates or travels in a UFO.

Ultrasonic - Pitches too high to be heard by humans.

Ultraviolet (UV) - Ultraviolet light is light from the upper end (long wave length/low frequency) of the electromagnetic spectrum. As with Infrared light, UV light is normally not visible to the naked human eye without the use of special viewing or photography equipment. Some paranormal investigators have experimented with using UV light to take video of ghosts and other paranormal entities. The results have been indeterminate. Other paranormal investigators have claimed UV light is an effective barrier to block demonic entities.

Umbanda - A Brazilian spirit religion.

Unction - anointing oil used in ceremonial magic.

Unicorn - A mythical horse-like creature with varying descriptions, but usually said to have a single horn on its forehead and possess magical powers.

Unidentified Flying Object (UFO) - This term is typically interpreted as "alien spaceship", although technically it simply means what it says — an object flying in the air which has not yet been identified.

Urban Legend - A story that is too good to be true and takes on a life of its own, usually told from the angle of "this happened to a friend of a friend." Paranormal urban legends include the vanishing hitchhiker, the devil baby and the hook and the boyfriend's death.

Vampire - Mythological or folkloric beings who subsist by feeding on the life essence (generally in the form of blood) of living creatures, regardless of whether they are undead or a living person. Although vampiric entities have been recorded in many cultures and according to speculation by literary historian Brian Frost that the "belief in vampires and bloodsucking demons is as old as man himself", and may go back to "prehistoric times", the term vampire was not popularized until the early 18th century, after an influx of vampire superstition into Western Europe from areas where vampire legends were frequent, such as the Balkans and Eastern Europe, although local variants were also known by different names, such as vampire in Serbia and Bulgaria, vrykolakas in Greece and strigoi in Romania. This increased level of vampire superstition in Europe led to mass hysteria and in some cases resulted in corpses actually being staked and people being accused of vampirism.

Vapor Apparition - A misty, white ghost.

VEP - Video Electronic Phenomena is a paranormal event captured on a camcorder or video.

Veridical - Information or experience that is confirmed by facts and events.

Veridical Dream - A dream that corresponds to real events past, present or future that are unknown to the dreamer.

Video Camera - This device is used for electronic motion picture acquisition. Solid-state images sensors (CCD) and subsequent CMOS active pixel sensors. A video camera either feeds real time images directly to a screen as output or archives them for further processing through optical disc media or computer memory. Signals are converted from analog-to-digital and/or digital-to-analog before they are presented as output. LCD produce near real-time representations of optical input and allow various editing functions. Video camcorders are extremely useful for investigators in the aspect that this technology can best represent and record any personal experience. Various light filters also increase the sensitivity of these devices (infrared, night vision).

Video Electronic Phenomena - VEP is a paranormal event captured on a camcorder or video.

Viles Vortices - A set of twelve points on a planetary grid that are said to be high in paranormal activity. Includes the Bermuda Triangle.

Vision - A psychic or religious incite.

Volt - A unit of electric potential and electromotive force (equal to the difference in potential needed to cause a current of one ampere to flow through a resistance of 1 ohm.

Voodoo - Magical practice considered to be a form of black magic but also is considered as a religion to some. Originating in Africa, and now found in Haiti, Jamaica and Cuba. Magical rites, trance states and possession.

Vortex, Vortices, Vortexes - A concentrated yet brief area of high electromagnetic energy often found in photographs taken at paranormally active locations. The often appear as sold (opaque) white or silver tubes, rods, or elongated ovals. They can also appear to be braided like a rope or chain (care has to be taken to ensure it is not a rope, chain, camera strap etc.). A vortex is not an entity. However, some paranormal researchers believe a vortex is a momentary doorway or portal to another realm that allows entities and other paranormal phenomena to come into our world. Some researchers also believe vortexes are linked to the Earth's own electromagnetic field which at least in part helps determine when these portals open/close. It is also believed that some locations are more prone to having active vortices due to the alignment of the Earth's magnetic field and local geological structure.

Waitoreke - These strange unknown otter-like beasts are seen in New Zealand, and as yet undiscovered.

Warlock - A male witch.

Warp - A location where the known laws of psychics do not always apply and space/time may be distorted. Two possible meanings:

1. Areas where conventional laws of physics can break down, linear time may not always apply. They can be locations infested with entities, imprints, and barrage of other paranormal activities. They may be unpredictable areas that can twist perceptions beyond the understanding of logic.

2. Areas of paranormal activity so intense that time itself changes. Time may speed up, slow down (Lost Time) or briefly stop altogether. The area effected is very small and of short duration.

Watt - Unit of power (equal to one joule per second.

Werewolf - A person who has been transformed into or having assimilated wolf-like characteristics.

Whammy - Casting a spell on another by staring intently, using direct eye contact, and influencing thoughts and behavior.

White Magic - Magical spells or rituals to produce beneficial effects without harm.

White Noise - A hiss-like sound, formed by combining all audible frequencies.

White Witch - A witch whose practice in witchcraft is solely for the purpose of good.

Whole Real - When you are able to document an experience both objectively and subjectively. There are three different types of whole real, 3 types.

1. When the subjective and the objective appear at the same time.

2. When the subjective and the objective appear at different times.

3. A combination of types I and II when the subjective and objective match but additional information is documented on either side.

Wicca - A duotheistic religion, worshipping a Goddess and a God, who are traditionally viewed as the Triple Goddess and Horned God. These two deities are often viewed as being facets of a greater pantheistic Godhead, and as manifesting themselves as various polytheistic deities. Nonetheless, there are also other theological positions within the Craft, ranging from monotheism to atheism. Wicca also involves the ritual practice of magic, largely influenced by the ceremonial magic of previous centuries, often in conjunction with a liberal code of morality known as the Wiccan Rede, although this is not adhered to by all Witches. Another characteristic of the Craft is the celebration of seasonally based festivals known as Sabbats, of which there are usually eight in number annually.

Wiccan - One who practices Wicca.

Wild Hunt - A group of ghost horsemen or packs of ghostly dogs seen at night.

Witch - A woman who practices witchcraft.

Witchcraft - The practice of performing acts with the aid of a spirit.

Witchdoctor - A medicine person or shaman who hunts down and fights "evil" Anthropologic Witches.

Witch finder - During the witch-hunts of the 16th and 17th centuries, a person hired to locate and identify witches. Since a fee was usually paid for finding a witch, impartiality was far from guaranteed.

Witching Hour - A slang term for the time of night when ghosts are the most active, usually placed at between midnight and 3 a.m.

Woo-Woo - People or ideas promoting unproven or pseudoscientific phenomena.

Wraith - An apparition of a living person that appears as a portent just before that person's death.

Xenoglossy - The ability to speak an unlearned foreign language.

Xenomancy - Divination by interpreting meetings with strangers.

Xing-Xing - This is a specific regional name, from southern China, for small unknown apes.

Xylomancy - A type of pyromancy (divination by fire), using burning wood.

Yara-ma-yha - Is said to be a 'merciless vampire' resembling a 'tiny toothless frog-man'. he lives and jumps down on his victims from trees in order to drain their blood.

Yeren - A mythical man beast or red haired ape 5-6 feet in height. Sighting of the Yeren have been reported in Asia and the Shennongjia Mountains in Central China. The Chinese Wildmen are reddish, semi-bipedal, and often encountered by locals and government officials along rural roads.

Yeti - Yeti, unknown rock apes, are creatures reported as crossing the Himalayan plateaus and living in the valley forests. There is not just "one" Abominable Snowman, and they are no white. Yoga - Religious philosophy originating in India. It advocates the use of physical and psycho-spiritual techniques to lead the person to higher consciousness and enhanced suppleness of body.

Yomie-Whowie - A legendary tall hairy unknown hominoids creature said to inhabit several remote areas of the Australian wilderness.

Zarcanor - A malevolent spirit which attacks people while they're asleep, inspiring nightmares, and sometimes even inflicting minor injuries such as scratches, bruises and what appear to be finger marks. The name is possibly of Slavic origin.

Zener Cards - A deck of cards containing five characters, used to test ESP abilities.

Zephyr - Spirit borne upon, governing, or manifesting as the western wind.

Zodiac - An imaginary band in the sky extending approximately 8° either side of the ecliptic (the apparent path of the Sun, Moon and planets).

Zombie - In Haitian and West Indian folklore, a soulless corpse reanimated by a voodoo priest. In popular Western culture, an un-dead creature that feeds on the flesh of humans, causing the victims to also become zombies.

Zooform Phenomena - A term coined by cryptozoologist Jonathan Downes which describes a supernatural creature resembling an animal.

Zoomancy - Divination though interpretation of the appearance and behavior of animals.

Zoomorphism - Representation of a deity or devil with animal attributes.

Demons or Daemon

-A-

Abaddon - (Hebrew) name for the Greek Apollyon, "angel of the bottomless pit". Abaddon has also been identified with the angel of death and destruction, demon of the abyss, and chief of demons of the underworld. In the Book of Revelation, he is identified as the chief of the demon locusts, which are themselves described as having the bodies of winged warhorses, the faces of humans, and the poisonous, curved tails of scorpions.

Abatu - An earth bound form of ground of destructive/negative energy in the Order of the Nine Angles. Associated with rites of the sacrifice. Is also known by another name of Sapanur.

Abdiel - (Arabic) Demon from "Abd" meaning slave. The lord of slaves/slavery. Also known as an angel who refused to join Satan's rebellion. In Hebrew you will find his name as the servant/messenger of God.

Abduxuel - (Enochian) Demon and is known as the demonic rulers of the lunar mansions.

Abigar - (Unk) Can fortell future and give military advice. One who rides a winged horse and knows the secrets of war.

Abigor - (Unk) A warrior demon who commands the infernal sixty legions. He has been named god of Grand Duke of Hell. Appears in a pleasant handsome cavalier form on winged horse.

Abraxas - Demon with the head of a king and snake-like feet, that holds a wip in his hands

Aclahayr - (Unk) Of the fourth hour of the Nuctemeron, Aclahayr is a genius spirit, bound of the fourth hour of the Nuctemeron, and who's mysteries wait to be discovered.

Adad/Addu - (Babylonian, Hittite) god of the storm/rain, also lord of abundance, the son of the god An, who's animal is the bull, and who's symbol is cluster of lightining flashes as he holds lightning bolts in his right hand, as the heaven and earth rise before him.

Addu/Adad - (Babylonian, Hittite) god of the storm/rain, also lord of abundance, the son of the god An, who's animal is the bull, and who's symbol is cluster of lightining flashes as he holds lightning bolts in his right hand, as the heaven and earth rise before him.

Ademon - is the siezer demon of the night, and is a manifestation of a person's soul.

Adramalech - (Samarian) devil. Commander of Hell. Wierius' chancellor of infernal regions. In Assyria where he was worshipped, children were supposedly burned at his alters. After the Israelite King, Hezekiah, was murdered by his two sons, Adramalech and Sharezer, as he was worshipping in the temple of his idol, Nisrach.

Adramelech - "king of fire" Grand Chancellor of the infernal empire, and in this role, presided over the Devils' general council. Is one of two throne angels along with Asmadai. He is also 8th of the 10 arch demons and a great minister/chancelor of the Order of the Fly, founded by Beelzebub. Was also under the supreme command of sammael, the venom of god. Often seen in the form of a mule or peacock.

Adriel - is a moon demon of the mansions by the Enochian traditions. demon of the Luna mansions works of hidden knowledge and sinister magick, but Still not much is known of Adriel, and who's mysteries wait to be discovered.

Adze - Vampire-like ghost of the people of Ewe from Ghana. He can obsess humans and sucks the blood of little children

Aeshma/Aesma - (Persian) One of seven archangels of the Persians. Has been recorded in history for at least three thousand years. Said to be a small hairy demon able to make men perform cruel acts. (Hebrew) devil of sensuality and luxury, originally 'creature of judgement'. He was the overseer of all the gambling houses in the court of Hell, and the general spreader of dissipation. This demon was adopted into the Hebrew mythology as Asmodeus. Also Asmodeus was the demon of lust, responsible for stirring up matrimonial trouble.

Aesma/Aeshma - (Persian) One of seven archangels of the Persians. Has been recorded in history for at least three thousand years. Said to be a small hairy demon able to make men perform cruel acts. (Hebrew) devil of sensuality and luxury, originally 'creature of judgement'. He was the overseer of all the gambling houses in the court of Hell, and the general spreader of dissipation. This demon was adopted into the Hebrew mythology as Asmodeus. Also Asmodeus was the demon of lust, responsible for stirring up matrimonial trouble.

Afrit - (Arabian) Ghost of the victim of a murder, that returns from the dead to take revenge on the murderer. It appears as smoke at the spot where the murder happened

Agaliarept - (Hebrew) Commander of armies of the second legion. General of hell - Grimoire of Pope Honorius. He controls the past and future and the power to discover all secrets, is especially good at stirring up enmity and distrust among men. He is one of the two demons directly under Lucifer. Agaliarept is one of the demon who is a ruler of Elelogap, who's governs matters connected with water.

Agares/Aguares/ Agreas - (Unk) is the demon of courage who can cause earthquakes, teaches languages, he find pleasure in teaching immoral expressions, he has power to destroy dignities, and is temporal and supernatural. He can make runaways come back, and those who run stand still. He is a duke or grand duke of hell but ruling in the eastern zones, and is being served by 13 legions of demons, one of 3 demons who serve lucifuge, prime minister of Lucifer.

Agathodemon - (Egyptian) is a flying serpents or dragons venerated by ancient people were also called Agathodemons, or more commonly known as good genies in the ancient Egyptians believed he has the shape of a serpent with the human head and he is a good spirit/demon and was worshiped

Agramon - (Unk) is the demon of fear and he stands at the end of the world in the Revelations

Agrat-bat-mahlaht - One of Satan's wives and she is a demoness/angel of whores and prostitutes

Ahazu - demon the siezer demon of the night

Ahpuch - (Mayan) is the god of death, king of metnal of the underworld as he was depicted to have a skeleton or corpse adorned with bells, he has the head of an owl, in Mexico and central Americans have believed that an owl's screeches would signify instant death.

Ahriman - (Mazdean) is a destructive spirit and the name given to fallen angels by the Persians.

Aka Manah - (Iranian) The arch-demon that causes bad mind, bad will and bad act.

Akatash - (Iranian) The arch-demon that creates evil. He tries, together with other demons, to destroy Zarathustra

Aku Aku - Demons of the Easter-Islands, that scare with their high and annoying voices

Alastor - (Unk) cruel demon called "the executioner" the avenger of evil deeds. Specifically, familial bloodshed. Is a personification of a curse, it especially by the tragic writers, to designate any deity or demon who avenges wrongs committed by men. He is in a class of evil spirits.

Aldinach - (Egyptian) A demon who causes natural disasters such as earthquakes, rainstorms, hailstorms, floods, hurricanes, tornados, and can sinks ships. He always assumed the shape of a woman.

Allocen/Alocer/Allocer - is a demon who appears in the form of a soldier, mounted on a great horse, his face like that of a lion, exceedingly red, his eyes flaming fire, his speech hoarse and loud. He is vary powerful demon, and the grand duke of Hades, ruler of 36 infernal legions, and is one of the 72 spirits of Solomon. He is said to teach astronomy and liberal arts but also to induce people to immorality, and provide very good familiars

Alperer - Ghost of the mountains in the region of the alps, that roams around because of the sins he has committed, and hunts lonely wonderers, scaring them to death

Alu-Demon - (Babylonian) is an ancient demon. He owns his parentage to a human being. He lies in wait for the unwary, and at night enters bed-chambers and terrorized people, threatening to pounce on them if they close their eyes He also hides himself in caverns and corners and slinks through the streets at night.

Amaimon - (Egyption) Sun God that is much like Lucifer except controls reproduction and life. The king of eastern portion of hell.

Amaymon - (Egyption) is a prince of hell, curious characteristic of this spirit, is shown during the Evocation of Asmodai to appearance, when the Exorcist must stand upright with his cap or headdress removed in a show of respect for if he dose not it is Amaymon who will deceive him and doom all his work. He has a deadly poisonous breath.

Amducias - Grand Duke of Hades. According to Wierius a demon of music

Amducious - (Hebrew) The destroyer

Ammit - (Egyptian) a female mixed being between crocodile, lion and hippo. It eats the souls that weren't allowed to go to the other world (heaven).

Ammon - (Egyption) Sun God. Much like Lucifer except controls reproduction and life

Amon - (Egyption) Sun God. Much like Lucifer except controls reproduction and life

Amoymon - (Egyption) Sun God. Much like Lucifer except controls reproduction and life

Amy - One of the 72 spirits of Solomon. Said to be supreme president of hell. He will trade knowledge for the human soul

Anamelech - (Assyrian) bearer of bad news. An obscure demon. His name means "good king". Some sources claim Anamelech is the moon goddess while Andramalech is the sun god

Andras - (Unk) god of quarrels. Grand marquis of hell.

Andrealphus - One of the 72 Spirits of Solomon. An infernal Marquis in the form of a peacock that teaches people astrology and commands 30 legions

Andrephalus - One of the 72 Spirits of Solomon. An infernal Marquis in the form of a peacock that teaches people astrology and commands 30 legions

Andromalius - One of the 72 Spirits of Solomon. Count of Hell in the form of a man, that punishes thieves and brings back stolen goods. He rules over 36 legions

Angra Mainyu - Evil ghost of torture and pain. He is the personification of the bad and the dark

Angrboda - The bringer of sorrow, a deamonic female Giant of the Edda, that conceived with Loki the Midgard-snake, Hel and Fenris, the wolf.

Anini - One of the 72 Spirits of Solomon

Ankou - Animal-shaped demon of death of the Bretagne that appears to old and sick persons, and is the keeper of the peace of the graves

Anneberg - (German) demon of mines

Anomylech - (Assyrian) bearer of bad news. An obscure demon. His name means "good king". Some sources claim Anamelech is the moon goddess while Andramalech is the sun god

Ansitif - (unk) Possessed Sister Barbara of St. Michael in 1643 during the possessions of the nuns at Louviers

Aosoth - Dark female force in the pantheon of the Order of the Nine Angles. Works of passion and death. The name should be vibrated

Apaosha - (Iranian) The demon of drought. He is riding a black, hairless horse

Apasmara - a dwarf-like demon, the personification of mindlessness and glare. He tries to hinder the Hindus from freeing themselves from the circle of reincarnation

Apollyn - (Greek) Another name for Satan

Apophis - (Egytian) A snake-shaped demon, that lives in the darkness as a gigantic snake and attacks the vehicle of the Sun-God in the morning and in the evening

Ardat-Lile - (Semitic) a female spirit/demon who weds human beings and wreaks havoc in the dwellings of men

Ariel - Demon of water from medieval times. His origins are in the koptic mythology

Arioch - (unk) Demon of vengence. He delivers vengence only when called on

Arphaxat - (Unk) The demon who possessed Loise de Pinterville during the possession of the nuns at Loudun.

Asag - (Sumerian) A demon that dries out the wells, covers the earth with wounds and distributes hi poison over them

Asakku - The cause of many plagues and pains

Asanbosam - These vampires have hooks for feet and come in three types (male, female, and child). They have iron teeth and dangles its feet down from the trees onto victims. Also sucks blood from the thumbs of sleeping people

Ashtaroth - (Phonician)- goddess of lust, seduction. Same as Ishtar. Turned male in christian mythology - Lord Treasurer of Hell. Prince of accusers and inquisitors. Demon of vanity and sloth. One of the 72 spirits of Solomon

Asmoday - (Persian) One of seven archangels of the Persians. Adopted later into Hebrew mythology as Asmodeus. Has been recorded in history for at least three thousand years. Said to be a small hairy demon able to make men perform cruel acts. (Hebrew) devil of sensuality and luxury, originally 'creature of judgement'. He was the overseer of all the gambling houses in the court of Hell, and the general spreader of dissipation. In addition, Asmodeus was the demon of lust, responsible for stirring up matrimonial trouble

Asmodeus - (Persian) One of seven archangels of the Persians. Adopted later into Hebrew mythology as Asmodeus. Has been recorded in history for at least three thousand years. Said to be a small hairy demon able to make men perform cruel acts. (Hebrew) devil of sensuality and luxury, originally 'creature of judgement'. He was the overseer of all the gambling houses in the court of Hell, and the general spreader of dissipation. In addition, Asmodeus was the demon of lust, responsible for stirring up matrimonial trouble

Aspis - Jewish being in the form of a snake, being the symbol of evil and stubbornness. One of this creature's ear is clogged with the end of his tail and holds it's other one on the earth in order not to hear sacred invocations

Astaroth - The mighty grand prince of hell. He teaches the free arts and commands 40 legions. He is known as the demon that regrets the rebellion of angels and considers himself innocent

Astarte - Queen of spirits of the dead

Astovidatu - (Iranian) The demon of death who hunts with Aeshma the souls of the dead

Aswang - Female vampire from the Philippinian Islands, that appears at daytime as a woman and at night as a flying monster that sucks the blood of sleeping persons or devours the shadows of people in order to kill them

Atazoth - The most powerful of the Dark Gods in the pantheon of the Order of the Nine Angles. The name itself signifies in one sense the purpose of the cosmic cycies and the opening of the Gates since 'Atazoth' as a word means 'an increasing of azoth.

Aulak - (Arabian) Terrible vampire that eats women and children

Avnas - President of hell that appears in the form of a blazing fire. He discovers treasures and commands 36 legions

Awar - Son of Iblis. Arab demon of laziness

Aym - (Unk) Grand duke of hell. Also Haborym

Aynaet- Female demon from Ethiopia. She is the personification of the Evil Stare

Ayperos - (Unk) Prince of hell. Subordinate in Grimoire of Pope Honorius

Az - (Iranian) Demon and personification of evil Longings

Azael - (Hebrew) god/demon of war. This demon is also a demon of the dessert. He also appears in the form of a billy-goat and is the leader of the Mala'ak (fallen angels, compare:Luzifer). Azazel also means scapegoat

Azanigin - Mother of all demons who lie waiting in Earth in the pantheon of the Order of the Nine Angles

Azathoth - Rules all time and space from a black throne at the center of Chaos

Azazel - (Hebrew) god/demon of war. This demon is also a demon of the dessert. He also appears in the form of a billy-goat and is the leader of the Mala'ak (fallen angels). Azazel also means scapegoat

-B-

Baal - General of the infernal armies, many peoples worship him with by sacrificing humans. His name means god or king

Baalberith - Infernal archivar and Master of the bound. He was called when the phoenizians swore oath

Baalphegor - The priests of the Moabitans sacrificed humans to him and shared their flesh with him. He keeps his mouth open to devour

Babi - (Egyptian) A monster that will eat the dead at the last trial

Bachbakuala-Nuksiwae - The man-eater of the northern end of the world. Deamonic being of the Kwaikiutl Indians. He eats the initiants

Bael - The demon on top of the infernal powers. He gives shrewdness and the art of invisibility. He is in command of 66 legions

Bajang - Blood-thirsty demon from Malaysia, that grows within the bodies of children born dead. He brings disease that lead to death

Baka - Demon from Haiti that comes as a returner to earth to eat human flesh

Balam, Balan - Terrible demon that commands 40 legions while riding naked on a bear. He can be asked about the past, the present and the future

Bana - (Hindu) Demon that is a friend of Shiva but also an enemy of Wishnu

Bannik - Demonical baths-ghosts which show the future to farmers' daughters who are ready to marry

Banshee - (gaelic Bean-Si) Irish bringer of death that produces loud sounds and screams of mourning to signify the death of a person

Baobhan-Sith - Scottish Vampire that appears as a pretty young girl dressed in green to attack young men and suck their blood

Baphomet - Baphomet was the demon that the temple-knights worshipped under islamic-occult influence. He is the embodyment of th dark side of the "great male prinicipal".

Bar Zangi - Demon of the desert from the mythology of the Kho-tribe in the Hindu region. He waylays hunters in order to kill them. When you cut off his head, it will grow back like a hydra

Barbados - Duke of the underworld in the form of a hunter that is able to predict the future from the sounds that animals make

Baron Samedi - Dark God of Death of the Neo-African Voodoo-cult. Appears in a topper and and all black

Basilisk - (Greek) Demonic animal whose breath, look, and bite kill instantly

Bathin - Demonic duke that has a snakes tail and knows all about herbs and gemstones. Also commands 30 legions

Beelzebub - (Christian) Beelzebub is the highest devil. He is insideous and mean. In jewish texts he is referred to as Lord of the Flies or of the feciespile

Befana - (Italian) Demon of the winter that roams around on cold winter nights punishes children who have been bad

Behemoth - A monster created by Jahwe that will be killed together with its sister Liwjatan in the last battle and served as food to the fair ones

Belial - Evil spirit of darkness, uselessness and desperation. He is the personification of the force against God

Belphegor - is a demon, and one of the seven princes of Hell, who helps people make discoveries. He seduces people by suggesting to them ingenious inventions that will make them rich. According to some 16th-century demonologists, his power is stronger in April

Bergmoench - Following a german tale, he is a demon in shape of a giant monk that mostly brings harm and trouble

Berith - Demon of lies and grand duke of hell. Betters the voice of singers and commands 26 legion

Beyrevra - (India) The head of the spirits in the air

Bhutas - Demonic spirits that suck blood and eat meat. They roam in the form of horses, pigs and giants

Bifrons , Bifrous - Count in the form of a monster and knows a lot about astrology. Commands 6 legions

Bilu - Man eating demons from Burma that appear human with sharp, tearing teeth and without a shadow which hunt their victims with great speed

Bilwis - (German) Consists of envy, meanity and disguise. Skinny in shape

Bisterk Ding - Water Demon from Hedgeloland. Described as black, wooly fur and gigantic eyed monster

Blutschink - Man-eating demon of the Tirolian mythology. He is a stalker that drinks blood from his victims and devours them

Bodach - Scottish ghost of the house. Lives in the highlands during and hides during the day in cimneys. Described as a old man whom is small and shrinky. Victimizes bad children whom don't like to sleep and pinches them everywhere, lifts their eyelids and causes them to have nightmares. This all stops when the child behaves good again

Boggart - Far relatives of the Bogies and Brownies which are mean little ghosts in the houses. Gnomelike little beings which are dark-skinned and dark haired and wear dirty rags as clothing. Pretty clumsy which causes them to make plenty of noise. Very mischievous, scare chickens, throw over milk containers, pinch sleeping babies on the nose, discharge clogs and other things of this nature. Most of the time, the only thing to do is to move out of the house to get rid of these pests

Bogie - English demon that steals children whom changes appearance and is known as the devil's assistant

Bohten Dayak - (Hindu) Demon similar to an imp that likes to play evil tricks and likes to cause rockslide

Bolla - (Albania) Demonic spirit that awakes on the day of St. George and eats whomever hit sees first

Botis - A count of hell that looks like a viper snake. He can reconcile friends and enemies and rules over 0 legions

Buda - (Ethiopia) Demons that are responsible for plagues, lack of fertility and children deaths

Buduh - (Arabian) Demon of love (female) from the group of Dschinns, whose services you may ask by simply writing down their names down with numbers or letters

Buer - Chairman of the underworld. He is in form of a star and teaches philosophy and logic, he is in command of 50 legions

Bune - Infernal duke in the form of a dragon with three heads and can grant people wealth. He is in command of 30 legions

Bushyasta - (Iranian) A demon long haired demon of lazyness and flabbyness. It hates all industrious and working people

Butz - Demonic Kobold, that leads hikers the in the wrong direction and creates trouble in houses. He also steals little children

Byleth - A king of hell. He isin command of 80 legions and is escorted by cats that blow a horn

Caacrinolas - Major chairman of the underworld which often appears as a dog can grant followers invisibility. Commands 36 legions

Cacus - Demon of ancient rome that spits fire and is the son of the god Vulcan. Lives in a cave and kills passerbys

Canaima - Demonic god of the Waika and Makiratare-indians. Has the ability to take any form/shape

Caym - Demon that shows in the form of a blackbird. The master os logic and pun and also commands 30 legions

Cham-Er - (Guatemala) Demon of death who appears as a skeleton and makes the final kill with a knife made from stone

Charmo Vetr - (Hindukusch) female demon of the Kam tribe that preys on travelers in misty valleys. She was soothed by sacrifices of animals

Charon - A Greek demon described to be a former God sent to the Underworld, he is said to be in charge of the Gates to the Underworld, opening them to the worthy or closing them and further abusing the damned, so they spend eternity in the dead lake/river of the Underworld, called the Styx. He has many forms, but he's mostly described as a bald, diseased man dressed in rags and sitting at the Gates of the Underworld. He's often depicted with a chain around his neck

Charun - The leader of the dead, the Keeper and torturer of the dead in the underworld. Often pictured as a mixture of many animals

Cherufe - (Chile/Argent.) Humongous being whom eats young girls

Chil Gazi - (Hunza) Demon that seduces woman, the husband of Yachemi

Chimaira - (Greek) Demonic half-breed of the underworld. This beast is special becuase of its three heads, one of a lion, one of a goat and one of a snake. Sister of Hydra and Kerberos

Chordeva - (India) female demon in shape of a cat for the Dravidian tribes. She visits the sick and consumes their food and causes death by licking their lips

Chumbaba - (Sumeric) Powerful Demon of nature of the Gigamesch-Epos. Embodys the evil and is the embodyment of an erupting vulcano

Chumur Deli - (Hindu) Demon who appears in the shape of a horse with iron legs and scares wanderes

Churel - (India) Ghost-vampires. Ugly demons that hate all life. They are created when a pregnant woman dies during Diwali

Cimejes - (Africa) Demon who rides on a black horse. He discovers long lost treasures and command 20 legions

Cluricauns - Ghosts that live in winecellars and pubs. They look like small barkeepers. They love alcohol and so are often drunk very often. The only possibility to get rid of them is to get rid of all of the alcohol in the house because it then gets too dry for them

Coatlicue - (Aztecs) Referred to as the :eater of everything" and possess a skirt of rattlesnakes

Cresil - Demon of impurity and laziness according to Christian demonic beliefs. He is the third in the order of the Thrones. Also known as Gressil

Crocell - Demon in the form of an angel that can create water and commands 48 legions

Curupira - (Amazon) Man-eating demon whom is a master of disguise, that is only noticable by his feet that are facing the opposite direction of that of a regular foot

Daevas - (Persian) The demons of addictive drunkenness, sexuality and envy. The cause of plagues, death and hunger. The hate religion and tempt the rightous

Daityas - (Hindu) they dwell in the underworld and disturb sacred sacrifices

Danag - (Philippines) Vampires that changed into vampires by drinking one drop of blood

Danglathas - (Hunza) Female demons that hunt humans and kill them, Sparks comefrom their eyes and they have great tusks

Dantalion - Infernal duke that appears as a man with many faces and can read minds. Commands 36 legions

Dearg-Due - (Irish) name meaning red blood-sucker. Female demon that once risen from her grave, seduces men and dooms them

Deber - Demon of pestilence mostly awake at night to attack and infect people

Decarabia - Demon that appears as a pentagram and has control over all birds. Commands 30 legions

Dengelmaennle - Alpine-meadow and Mountain ghost whose sounds announce a human's passing

Deumos - Demon who is the deity of the locals of Calicut, Malabar. This demon has four horns and is a human soul devourer

Deumus - Demonical deity of the inhabitants of Calicut in Malabar. He has four horns and devours the souls of humans

Diablos - (Greek) Roams the earth to tempt christian people. Also, the antagonist of the Archangel Michael (sometimes the same as Satan).

Dialen - Female demons that have goatfeet from Graubuenden. They like humans and help them with their work or present gifts to them

Dibbuk - (Jewish) Evil spirits that cause mental illnesses, rage and other changes in personality

Dimme - (Sumerian) The female demon of the fevor after childbirth and the sicknesses of babies

Diwo - (Hindu) Desease spreading demon that takes the shape of a dog. It can breath fire and will pounce on people in order to bring its paralyzing touch

Djinn - (Arabian) Demons of the dessert, the embodyment of the negative and aggresive nature. They appear as miscellanious animals and humanoids

Dogai - Female ugly spirits from the melanesian-papuanian Torres-indians. They kidnap boys and young men to live with them

Dowadiru - (Hindu) Giant demon of the dessert that is always sourrounded by fire and has a horn on his forehead, seeks to frighten people

Drak - (German) Little imp from central Germany, that appears in the form of a firy dragon and usually lives in houses. If you treat the drak well, he will steal gold, jewelry or food for you

Dre - (Tibet) the bringers of death and stand for everything harming

Drude - Female alb that causes fearfull dreams with the feelings of suffocation

Druj - (Iran) Female Archdemon of lie, causes a lot of evil with unclean men and calls bad things good

Duppy - (West Indian) Causes through touch the worst deceases

-E-

Eurynome - In the Pelasgian version of the Greek creation myth, Eurynome is the name of the primal mother of the gods and dancing creatrix of the universe, who ruled Olympus as queen with her son and husband, the Titan Ophion who had the form of a great serpent. Eurynome means "wide wandering." In the shape of a dove she laid the cosmic egg containing all things in the universe. When Ophion coiled around the egg seven times, it broke into two and released the sun, moon, planets, stars, mountains, rivers, and living creatures

-F-

Focalor - has power over the winds and the sea and causes ships to sink and death by drowning. He will not hurt anyone or thing, if asked not to

Furfur aka Furtur - is a powerful Great Earl of Hell ruling over twenty-nine legions of demons. He is a liar unless complelled to enter a magic triangle where he gives true answers to every question, speaking with a rough voice. Furfur causes love between a man and a woman, creates storms, tempests, thunder, lighting and blasts. Also known to teach on secret and divine things

-G-

Gaap - is the mighty Prince and Great President of Hell in command of sixty-six legions of demons. According to the Lesser Key of Solomon, the king and prince of the southern region of Hell and Earth. According to the Pseudomonarchia Daemonum (False Monarchy of Demons) the king of western region and as mighty as Beleth. He is said to be better conjured to appear when the Sun is in a southern zodiacal sign.Gaap specifically commands the element of water and reigns over the Water Elementals or the "water demons"

Geryon - had three heads and three bodies with a total of six arms. The three bodies were joined to one pair of legs, but apart from this weird feature, his appearance was that of a warrior. He owned a two-headed houndnamed Orthrus, which was the brother of Cerberus, and a herd of magnificent red cattle that were guarded by Orthrus, and a man named Eurythion

Haures - She destroys and burns enemies of the mage and kills men by fire and protects the mage against other spirits. She knows all secrets and will bring harm to one's foes. Haures is female. Her golden hair can turn to blood red. She has large eyes that match her hair, there is no white in them at all. She is a beautiful demoness. She is very fair skinned with long legs and thinly built. She is rather calm and quiet. She floats on the air. She appeared without wings

-I-

Iblis - (islamic devil) The leader of the Djinns. Once he was banned from Paradise. He lives in ruins and graveyards

Illuyanka - (hethitic) Dragon-like snake. It defeated the god of thunderstorms, Teshup, and took his heart and his eye

Imdugud - (sumerian) Demonical mix-being, that threatens domestic animalsin shape of an eagle with the head of a lion

Impundulu - Demon of people from the region of the Cape of South Africa, that lives off blood and brings decease and death

Incubus Incubus aka Incubi - (Latin the ones that lie on you) They are male nightmares, ghosts that sit on the sleepers chest and cause nightmares. They are also lovers of witches, and the male counterpart to succubi, energy sucking spirits of sexual lusting. A demon in the male form who lie on women in order to have sex with them. Its female counterpart is the succubus. An incubus may pursue sexual relations with a woman in order to father a child, as in the legend of Merlin. Religious traditions foretells that repeated intercourse with an incubus or succubus may result in the deterioration of health or even death

Indra - (iranian) Archdemon and the disparaged version of the hindi god Indra. Hates the truth and animates men to fight

Inguma - (baskian) Evil spirits of the night that comes to people, grabs their throat and causes them fear

Ipes - Duke of hell, appears in the form of a lion and gives his followers courage. He is in command of 36 legions

Ipos - Demon count of hell who commands 36 legions; looks like a lion-headed angel. Ipos (Ipes) appears as an angel or lion with the head and feet of a goose and a short rabbit's tail. Ipes knows the past and future, gives men intellect and courage, and can tell the location of hidden treasures

Iya - Indian monster and embodyment of the evil for the Lakota-Indians. His breath brings sickness and he eats animals and humans

-J-

Jahi - The poisoner. She is a female devil that waked Angra Mainyu from his sleep. As a reward she recieved a kiss because of which she got the period and thus a husband

Jaldabaoth - Gnostic spiritual being, lord of the underworld. He raped the first woman and seduced thus the first humans into sexual intercourse

Jeretik - Demonical undead of the Russian Mythology. They appear in tattered appearance and spread bad weather, droughts and plagues

Jestan - The demonic chief from the Hindukusch Mythology. Jestan causes desease, famine and war. He often appears in the shape of a dog

Jezebeth - Demon of falsehoods and lies

Jigarkhvar - Female demon of the indian mythology. She makes people faint though her look and takes out their liver and eats it

Joetun - Embodyment of the unlimited natur of the german mythology. A giant and being of chaos, also known as devourer

-K-

Kasdeya - According to The Book of Enoch (LXIX:12) "the fifth Satan"

Kobal - Entertainment Director of Hell, patron of comedians. Demon of hilarity

-L-

Leonard - Often called "le Grand Negre" (The Black Man), Leonard is demon of the first order, grand master of the sabbaths, chief of the subaltern demons, and inspector general of sorcery, black magic and witchcraft. From the waist up, Leonard has a goat's body with 3 horns on his head, a goat's beard, hair-like bristles, 2 ears like foxes, and inflamed eyes. He also has a face on his butt, which witches kiss while holding a green candle to adore him. Leonard can take the form of a bloodhound, a beef, a black bird, or a tree trunk with a gloomy face. When he attends the sabbath, he has the feet of a goose, although experts claim that he has no feet when in tree trunk form. Leonard's attitude is reserved and melancholic, but when he appears at witch and devil assemblies, he is commanding and uses situations to his advantage

Leviathan - Leviathan was a large whale-like sea creature, who may have had 7 heads according to some legends. A lengthy description of him comes from the "Book of Job"

Lilith - Appealing to both magicians and feminists past and present, Lilith, or Lilitu ("wind-spirit" in Assyrian-Babylonian mythology) was a ravenous sexual entrepreneur. In legend, Lilith was the first wife of Adam. She was either created as Adam's Siamese twin (joined together at the back), or was made from filth. Either way, Lilith demanded equality with Adam

Lucifer - "Lucifer" generally refers to the Devil, although the name is not applied to him in the New Testament. Post-New Testment Lucifer is often used as the name of the Devil and often thought as the Devil's name before he fell from Heaven

-M-

Malphas - Malphas is a Great President and a Prince to some authors, having forty legions of demons under his command.

Malphas - is depicted as a crow that after a while or under request changes shape into a man, and speaks with a hoarse voice.

Malphas - builds houses, high towers and strongholds, throws down the buildings of the enemies, can destroy the enemies' desires or thoughts (and/or make them known to the conjurer) and all what they have done, gives good familiars, and can bring quickly artificers together from all places of the world. Malphas accepts willingly and kindly any sacrifice offered to him, but then he will deceive the conjurer

Mammon - Mammon is a term from the Christian Bible used to describe material wealth or greed, most often personified as a deity

Mastema - Mastema "hostility" is the name of an arch-demon and chief of the demons engendered by the fallen Watcher/Angels with women, perhaps on of those same demons. His actions and name indicate he is Satan, the 'Adversary', but much more the Satan who appears in the book of Job with a function to fulfill under God than the Satan of later tradition who is the uttermost enemy of God. Beliar, mentioned twice in Jubilees, is likely to be identical with Mastema in this work

Melchom - This name is possibly derived from Milcom, the god of the Ammonites, so there may be a connection to Moloch.

Melchom - is the paymaster of civil servants in hell. He is known as the demon who carries the purse

Mephistopheles Mephistopheles (also Mephistophilus, Mephistophilis, Mephostopheles, Mephisto and variants) - is a demon featured in German folklore. He originally appeared in literature as the demon in the Faust legend, and he has since appeared in other works as a stock character version of the Devil himself

Merihim - Merihim is the demon prince of pestilence

Moloch - Moloch, whose name probably derived from Melech "king" and Bosheth, "shame", was one of the deities worshipped by the idolatrous Israelites. He was referred to as "the abomination of the children of Ammon" (1 Kings 11:7) and the primary means of worshipping him appears to be child sacrifice or "to pass through the fire." Solomon was said to have built a temple to him

Mullin - Demon lieutenant of the demon Leonard

Murmur - Great Duke, comes with trumpets sounding and rules 30 legions

-N-

Naberius Cerbere/ Cerberus/ Naberus - is a strong and powerful demon commanding 29 legions. One of the marquis of hell. Cerberus appears as a three headed dog or a raven. He has a raucous voice but presents himself as eloquent and amiable. He teaches the art of gracious living

Nergal - The name Nergal, Nirgal, or Nergali (Hebrew) refers to a diet in Babylon. Nergal is mentioned in the Hebrew bible as the diety of the city of Cuth (Cuthah). He is the son of Enlil and Ninlil

Nicor - Water demon known for drowning humans; can cause hurricanes, tempests and the like

Nybbas - Nybbas is a demon or spirit in the Dictionnaire Infernal that manages visions and dreams. He is regarded as a fool and jester. He is depicted as smiling. He is of the inferior order, high upper gallery of hell

135

Nysrogh - Chief of the House of Princes of Hell, a second order demon

-O-

Oriax - The Fifty-ninth Spirit is Oriax, or Orias. He is a Great Marquis, and appeareth in the Form of a Lion,26 riding upon a Horse Mighty and Strong, with a Serpent's Tail; and he holdeth in his Right Hand two Great Serpents hissing. His Office is to teach the Virtues of the Stars, and to know the Mansions of the Planets, and how to understand their Virtues. He also transformeth Men, and he giveth Dignities, Prelacies, and Confirmation thereof; also Favour with Friends and with Foes. He doth govern 30 Legions of Spirits; and his Seal is this, etc

Ornias - Ornias (meaning "pesky") is the first demon mentioned in the Testament of Solomon. This demon was bothering the head workman's son as they were constructing the Temple of Jerusalem. Every day at sunset, the demon would take half of the boy's pay and drain his energy. Solomon became curious as to why the boy was growing thinner, and upon learning of demon's tasks, he began to pray to God that he would grant him authority over the demon. God heard Solomons' prayers and sent the archangel Michael to deliver a ring to Solomon with the seal of God. This ring would be able to imprison demons and force them to help construct the great Temple of Jerusalem. Solomon gave the ring to the boy and instructed him to throw the ring into the demon's chest and command him to go to Solomon when the demon appeared that day. The boy followed the commands of Solomon and Solomon questioned the demon Ornias

Ose - is a Great President of Hell, ruling three legions of demons (thirty to other authors, and Pseudomonarchia Daemonum gives no number of legions). He makes men wise in all liberal sciences and gives true answers concerning divine and secret things; he also brings insanity to any person the conjurer wishes, making him/her believe that he/she is the creature or thing the magician desired, or makes that person think he is a king and wearing a crown, or a Pope.

Paymon - A demon king of hell, master of ceremonies; governs 200 legions

Philatanus - Demon who assists Belial in sodomy and pedophile behaviors

Proserpine - A demon who likes to assist Belial in sodomy

Pruflas - A demon high prince and grand duke of hell, Pruflas/Busas commands 26 legions. In Babylon, where he shall reign, he has the head of an owl. Pruflas facilitates quarrels and wars, provokes discord, and generates poverty. He will respond to all he is asked to do

Pyro - (Unk) Ademon prince of falsehood

-Q-

Quingo - (Akkadian) Lord of the demons that was defeated by Marduk, out of his blood humans were created

-R-

Raum - A Count of Hell who commands thirty legions of demons

Rimmon - Also known as Damas, is the Ambassodor of Hell for Russia

Ronove - Ronove teaches languages. He humbles enemies and teaches art and rhetoric. He also provides servants.Ronove has brilliant shoulder-length golden hair that shines and glitters, with a brilliant aura. He has markings on his face like a tribal warrior. He has a very small wingspan. He can move objects in a room and is very talkative and friendly. He sometimes goes by the name "Ben." He is a Demon of fire and specializes in pyrokinesis. He gives off a lot of energy and also specializes in languages

Ronwe - Commands nineteen legions of devils in Hell

-S-

Samael - Samael (Hebrew) (also Sammael, perhaps "Venom of God") is an important archangel in Talmudic and post-Talmudic lore, a figure who is accuser, seducer and destroyer, and has been regarded as both good and evil. It is said that he was the guardian angel of Esau and a patron of the empire of Rome. Also called Sammael and Samil, he is considered in legend both a member of the heavenly host (with often grim and destructive duties) and a fallen angel, equatable with Satan and the chief of the evil spirits. One of Samael's greatest roles in Jewish lore is that of the angel of death. In this capacity he is a fallen angel but nevertheless remains one of the Lord's servants. As a good angel, Samael supposedly resides in the seventh heaven, although he is declared to be the chief angel of the fifth heaven

Semiazas - Chief demon of fallen angels

Shabriri - Known as the demon who made people go blind

Shax - Shax is a Great Marquis (and a Duke to some authors) of Hell with thirty legions of demons under his command.

Shax - is depicted as a stork that speaks with a hoarse but subtle voice; his voice changes into a beautiful one once he entered the magic triangle.

Shax - takes away the sight, hearing and understanding of any person under the conjurer's request, and steals money out of kings' houses, only to return it 1200 years later if everything is still in order. He also steals horses and everything the conjurer asks. Shax can also discover hidden things if they are not kept by evil spirits, and sometimes gives good familiars, but sometimes those familiars deceive the conjurer. If he is confined to a triangle, he will speak truth on supernatural matters, point out hidden treasures not guarded

138

by evil spirits, and obey the exorcist. If he is not confined, he will lie and not always obey the exorcist

Sonneillon - Demon of hatred

Stolas - Stolas is a high prince of hell commanding 26 legions. He appears as an owl or as a man who teaches astronomy, the properties of plants, and the worth of precious stones

Succorbenoth - The demon of jealousy

-T-

Thamuz - Ambassador of hell, demon master of big weapons

-U-

Udl - Flying demon from Austria. He tells about war and bad luck by his cries

Udug - (Sumer) Demons that used to be guardians, but degenerated into demons

Uezuet - Demonical souls of the dead of the Tatars. They are known to be greedy, and come into the bodies of people to cause stomachache

Uhaml - Demonical bird from Austria. He announces bad luck with his shouts

Ukobach - Stationary Engineer of Hell, Inventor of Fireworks

Ukopach - Demon of lower rank whose body is red. He is the inventor of fireworks. Beelzebub ordered him to watch over the fires of hell

Umi Bozu - Giant demon of the sea from Japan. He threatens ships

Ummar - Evil spirits from the Qur'an that can spoil magical work

Uphir - Head of the HMO of Hell, Demon physician and apothecary

Uvall - Uvall reveals past, present, and future. He reconciles enemies and brings the love of a woman to a man. He creates friendships and ensures esteem. He knows all and can manipulate time.

Uvall - is a unisex Demon. She/He has long flowing blonde curly hair, deep green eyes, is very tall and is built stocky. Her/His name is pronounced "Ewe-Val". Uvall wears golden body armor and has white wings

-V-

Vajrapani - Cruel lord of the demons from Tibet, that is known for his terrible deeds

Valafar - Grand Duke of Hell "in charge" according to Tondriau and Villeneuve (1972).

Valefor - A duke in the form of a lion with the head of a donkey. He commands 10 legions

Vampires - (slavic) Vampires are demons and ghosts of the dead. They suck the blood of their victims until they are dead. See the Vampires Section for more details

Vanth - (etruskia) Female demon of the underworld and the dead. She is the bringer of death and helps the dieing

Vapula - Duke of hell in the form of a lion that teaches people different crafts and philosophy. He is in command of 36 legions

Vassago - Aprince of Darkness. He tells of the past and the future. He is in command of 26 legions

Vaya - (iranian) Demon of wind and death that causes death numbing the body and fights for possessing the soul

Vepar - Demonic duke that can call storms and makes people die of gangrene. He appears in shape of a mermaid and is in command of 29 legions

Verdelet - The demon who carries witches to Sabbath

Verin - is the demon of impatience. His adversary is St. Dominic. It is said that Verrine tempts man with impatience and motivates them to action. He is one of the nine demonic divinities written in the black book around 1312 AD. In the divinities he is considered the positive polarity; where Amducious is the negative polarity. In the divinities Verrine , Lucifer, and Leviathan take on the feminine aspect

Vetis - A demon of hell who corrupts and tempts the holy

Vila - Ghosts of the woods in slavic mythology. They cause disorientation and attack wanderers

Vine - Demonic king in the form of a lion. He causes storms and makes walls break down. He commands 36 legions

Virikas - Little abominable demons from India. They scare people with their screams

Virolac - Were-being from the romanian mythology, that eats the stars

Vishap - Armenian ghost of the thunderstorm that carries away the fruits of harvest. A spear put into his blood is indestructable and absolutely deadly

Vodnik - Froglike demon of nature of the slavic belief, that waits on the shores of swampy rivers and pulls people into his world

Voval - Grand chairman of the underworld. He appears in the form of a child with angelwings and shows the locations of planets. He has 30 legions

Vrita - Infernal duke in the form of a dromedary that can make women fall in love and is in command of 37 legions

Wall - Powerful duke of hell. He appears as a dromedary and knows the past and the future. 36 legions serve him

Wasco - Demonical mix-being from the records of the Nutka-indios. The Wasco catches little children and devours them

Wendigo - Demon of the woods from Canada, that hunts humans and eats the flesh of his victims

Were-beings - (lycanthropes) Were-beings can be found in any culture. The most commonly known are the werewolves. They are the mirror of the human and the animal side within us

Werzelya - Female demon from Ethiopia that killed her daughter and drank her blood

Wichan Alwe - Evil souls of the dead of the Araukanians, They drill a hole to the heart of their victims and suck their blood

Wolba - Evil demons of the wind of the australian Aboriginals. With their huge fangs they bite humans and make their skin tear or poison them

Wraith - Scottish ghost. Everybody who meets him will die soon

Wrukolas - Vampires from the Aegaeis Islands. He strangles his victims and then kills them

Wutr - Ugly female demons (women of the Yush) that feast on humans

-X-

Xaphan - Demon of lower class. Xaphan suggested to set heaven on fire, was banished to hell and is now responsible for the glowing of coal

Xastur - Kills people while they sleep and devours the dead

Xhinde - (Albania) Evil, elflike ghosts. They show their appearance slamming doors and flickering light

Xolotl - The destructive Twin-Sister of Quetzacoatl, she embodys the dark side of the aztecian belief and she embody's the evening-star

Xtabai - Demons of the Maya. They bring decease, abduct people into the underworld or throw them into holes in the ground

-Y-

Yachemi Anthropophagous - female demon (Hindukusch) that attacks wanderers and devours half of them

Yama - Ancient indians god of death, that pulls the soul out of a dead body with a snare

Yama-Onna - Threatfull with of the mountains in the ancient japanese mythology. She is incredibly greedy and devours people

Yamale - Huge demons that live in caves (Hindukusch) that hunt humans and eat them up

Yan-Gant-Y-Tan - Bretonical demon, a wanderer in the night. Meeting him means and evil omen

Yara-Ma-Yha-Who

Yatsh - Giant one-eyed demons from the region of Pamir. The Yatsh ravage fields because they despise agriculture

Yipon - Hunting-demon from the region above the karawari-river in Guinea. He has the figure of a wild boar and bring the luck for the hunt

Ymir - Demonical giant, the forefather of the Rife-Giants. The first living beings evolved out of the sweat of his armpits. When the gods killed him, they created all wateron earth out of his blood and the earth out of his flesh

Yukki-Onna - Female Japanese demon of snow and ice. She makes sleeping people freeze to death when she touches them with her icy breath

Yush - Giant red demons that have hands with six fingers on them from the Kafir mythology. They hunt humans in order to devour them

-Z-

Zaebos - Grand Count of the Underworld/Infernal Realms that appears as a handsome soldier and rides on a crocodile

Zagan - King of hell in the form of a bull that can turn water into wine and make a wise man out of a fool. He is in command of 33 legions

Zarich - (Iranian) Archdemon that makes people get old

Zepar - Infernal duke that appears in the form of a soldier that either brings people together in love or makes them infertile.He is in command of 60 legions

Zipacna - Demon of earthquake of the Maya. He appears in shape of a giant

Zmeu - Romainian vampires, that enter the sleeping rooms of young women at night and seduce them

Zombie - Most popular from the Voodoo-cult of Haiti in which the dead is reanimated and don't feel pain. Zombies have existed for hundreds, perhaps thousands, of years, in the form/brought of magical or religious ceremonies which raised the dead.

Zombology - Took form about 1912. In 1912, Dr. Otto Standish, known as the Father of Modern Zombology, published "Mechanisms and Characteristics of the Undead", a treatise which raised zombology from the level of folklore and myth to a science. Dr. Otto Standish spent several years in the field studying the Voodoo rituals which produced the undead, and their effects on undead physiology

Zu Akkadian - Demon appearing as a bird of storms, personification of the southwind. He stole the tables of fate from Elil to make himself the highest god

Zupay - For the Inka the personification of bad violence, that tortures the souls in hell

Gemstones and Crystals

Gemstones and Crystals are one of the most beautiful, mystical and profound "energy medicine" tools, which have been used for centuries throughout all cultures, religions and empires. Crystals bring amazing benefits to the healing.

Some gemstones and crystals have long-standing traditional uses and properties while others may have newer discoveries of uses or properties. Always follow the guidance and wisdom of the Divine and of your higher self when working with gemstones and crystals.

All gemstones and crystals should be cleansed and charged before use. This can be done by placing the gemstone or crystal in pure running water, such as a stream for a few minutes. Some say they should be cleansed with each of the four elements in turn, fire being very brief to prevent damage to the gemstone or crystal. The process of charging will depend upon you, some people will use sunlight, and others will use moonlight. Both methods however, involve placing the gemstone or crystal in the chosen light source for a period of time. The greater the amount of cleansing and charging time required.

Agate

1. Banded Agate - Used for protection, to restore energy within the body and relieve stress.

2. Black Agate - Used for protection, worn to enhance personal courage and aid success in competitive endeavors.

3. Black and White Agate - Used as an amulet to guard against physical dangers.

4. Blue Agate - Used as an amulet to promote peace and happiness. Can be used to de-stress yourself by holding in your hand.

5. Brown (tawny) Agate - Used as an amulet to aid success in virtually any undertaking, can also be used as a wealth talisman.

6. Green Agate - Used to promote healthy eyesight.

7.   Moss Agate - Used as a talisman by gardeners to ensure "green fingers". It is also used for the relief of aches and pains, especially neck ache.

8.   Red Agate (Blood agate) - Used to promote calm and inner peace, it can also be used to heal the blood and guard against insect bites.

Amazonite - Used to attract money and bring good luck, hence the gambling connection. It is also widely used to heal emotional problems and to mend the aura.

Amber - Is neither a gemstone nor a crystal, but is fossilized resin of pine trees, as such it frequently contains insects, and is therefore seen as a giver of life energy. Amber also represents the Goddess or Great Mother, and is sometimes worn by Witches in a necklace of alternating amber and jet (representing the God) beads. It is used to enhance magical ability and to ward off negativity, whether it is within your own spells or of those directed against you. Be wary of being fobbed off with imitation amber. Fake amber it is made of glass or plastic, true amber is warm to the touch, smells slightly of pear drops, and produces a sweet smelling smoke if you push a hot pin into it (plastic smells pungent and acidic).

Amethyst - Use to prevent insomnia and nightmares by sleeping with a piece of amethyst under your pillow. It is a reducer of stress, so it can be used to great effect in today's pressured lifestyle. Use amethyst to calm fears, raise hopes, and enhance spirituality. Amethyst can also be used to enhance psychic abilities, and aid meditation. An all-round gemstone that you should not be without.

Aquamarine - Used to purify the body before ritual, as a protective amulet when travelling over water, to sooth emotional problems, and to enhance the use of psychic powers.

Aventurine - Worn as an amulet to improve eyesight, increase perception, and to enhance intelligence. Gamblers also use it as a lucky talisman (keep your lottery ticket under a piece of aventurine!).

Azurite - Used to increase psychic powers. Place a piece beneath your pillow at night for dreams of revelation. It is also useful as and aid during divination.

Bloodstone - Used in ancient times by soldiers to stem the flow of blood, this stone has blood-healing properties. It can also be used in spells associated with wealth and business/legal matters, and as a talisman to increase crop yield.

Calcite

1. Orange Calcite - Used as a meditation focal point.

2. Pink Calcite - Used for centering and grounding, and for love rituals.

3. Blue Calcite - Used for purification.

4. Green Calcite - Used for financial prosperity.

5. Orange Calcite - Used to promote protective energy.

Carnelian - Worn to calm anger and aggression, also to give courage when speaking in public. It is used to help prevent others from reading your mind, to strengthen astral vision, and to increase sexual desires.

Chrysocolla - Used to sooth the emotions, and promote loving relationships.

Citrine - Used to prevent nightmares and promote quality sleep. It is also used to enhance psychic ability, and to increase self-esteem.

Fluorite - Used to increase the mental faculties, and as a strengthener to increase the power of other stones. It can also be used to promote inner peace whilst meditating.

Hematite - Is used to cure some diseases or problems. It makes your heart and soul calmed down, and provides you with balance in life. It helps people understand better certain perspectives and keeps you humbled and down to earth. You become practical when you have the stone, and it improves your mentality. It pushes you to meditate making you improve your relationship with family and friends. And most of all, it provides you satisfaction and inner happiness.

Iron Pyrite (Fools gold) - Used by crystal healers to help with addiction problems and lung/breathing complaints. This stone was used by Mexican Indians to produce magic mirrors.

Jasper

1. Red Jasper - Used to return negative energy to the sender.

2. Green Jasper - Used as a health talisman, and to promote quality sleep.

3. Brown Jasper - Used for centering and grounding after magical rituals.

4. Mottled Jasper - Used for protection against drowning.

Jet - Black fossilized wood, sometime called Witches' amber. Used to absorb negative energies, to prevent nightmares, and to aid divination. Witches sometimes wear it in a necklace of alternating amber (representing the Goddess) and jet beads.

Lapis Lazuli - used with other stones when parts of the body need to be purified and cleansed and should be only used by a healer. Lapis Lazuli has high intensity and can open many of the chakra centers. This must be done only with love in the heart and comprehension in the mind and wisdom in soul.

Malachite - Used to increase your sending power during rituals.

Obsidian - Often cut into polished flat sheets for use as a scrying mirror.

Onyx - Be wary of having too much onyx in the house as it can reduce your sexual desires to a dangerously low level, thus preventing the natural release of emotional energies.

Quartz

1. Quartz Rose Quartz - Used to unblock energy centers and aid the body's natural healing process. It is also used in the tips to wands, as a scrying tool, and as representations of the God and Goddess on the altar. There however hundreds of other uses for this versatile crystal.

2. Blue Quartz - Used to promote peace and tranquility.

3.   Green Quartz - Used to increase wealth.

4.   Rose Quartz - Used to open the heart chakra, and to promote peace and harmony.

5.   Rutilated Quartz - Used to increase personal energy during rituals.

6.   Smokey Quartz - Used for grounding, and to overcome depression.

7.   Tourmaline Quartz - Used to aid astral projection if placed under the pillow at night.

Ruby - Can be used for scrying, attracting wealth, and promoting happiness.

Sodalite - Used to reduce stress levels and lower blood pressure.

Sugilite - Used during meditation to increase spiritual awareness.

Tigers Eye - Used to increase self-confidence, and to counteract stress related problems.

Tourmaline

1.   Pink Tourmaline - To attract lovers and promote friendship.

2.   Red Tourmaline - Used to increase personal energy during rituals, and to increase courage.

3.   Green Tourmaline - Used to attract wealth and stimulate creativity.

4.   Blue Tourmaline - Used to reduce stress.

5.   Black Tourmaline - Used to absorb negativity.

6.   Watermelon Tourmaline - Used to balance the energies within the body.

7.   Tourmaline Quartz - Used to aid astral projection if placed under the pillow at night.

1. Howlite Turquoise - Used to relieve insomnia, balances calcium levels and strengthens teeth and bones.

Candle Color Meaning

For decades candles of different colors have been burned in rituals to attract desired emotions, material wealth, or karma and can be one of the most effective tools used for meditation, rituals and other ceremonies. With a relaxed, positive state of mind, burn the candle color that best influences your motivation and think about what you want to accomplish.

With knowledge and Understanding in Candles, Colors, and their meanings you can accomplish many great things for yourself and achieve what you once thought was impossible.

Black - Used in rituals to induce a deep meditational state, to protect and/or to ward off negativity. Can be used to banish evil or negativity as in uncrossing rituals; attracts Saturn energy. Burning black with any other color is said to dissolves all negative energies.

Blue - The primary spiritual color It's used to obtain wisdom, harmony, inner light, or peace; confers truth and guidance. Other uses include healing, sleep, creativity, perception, calming wisdom, truth, loyalty, dreams, and the examination of emotions. Some say it represents the divine mother.

Blue (Dark) - Promotes laughter and joy as well as loyalty. Can be used to attract Jupiter energy, or whenever an influence needs to be increased. Confers wisdom and self-awareness. Can be calming and assist sleep. Also used to influence truth, dreams, emotions, and loyalty.

Blue (Light) - Another very spiritual color: it is used to increase peace, tranquility, patience, and calmness. It radiates Aquarian energy and can be used in devotional or inspirational meditations; employ where a situation must be synthesized.

Blue (Royal) - Mostly used to confer wisdom, protection, and good fortune. Increases spiritual awareness. Also increases communication, which can cause change. Can bring about a deep meditational state. Used in rituals that need increased Saturn energy.

Brown - This is an earthy, well-balanced color It is used for rituals of material increase. It is said to eliminate indecisiveness and improve powers of concentration, study, and/or telepathy. Said to increases financial success.

Also represents the home. Some say those born under Capricorn will be more potent in their work using it.

Gold - Fosters understanding and is said to bring about fast luck or money. Represents solar energy. It is used to heal all inner wounds, also to confer money smarts. Prosperity, wealth, money, attraction. Some also say it represents enlightenment, protection and the Divine Mother.

Green - Promotes prosperity, fertility, and success. Stimulates good luck, can increase money, harmony, and rejuvenation. Also represents Healing, health, and growth. Can be an important component in rituals involving Venus; attracts love, and social delights.

Green (Dark) - Color of ambition, greed, and jealousy, used to counteract these influences in a ritual. Also relates to personal goals.

Gray - Useful when pondering complex issues, can also neutralize negative influences without repercussions. Represents balance, encourages stability, helps develop psychic abilities. In magic, this color often sparks confusion; it also can negate or neutralize a negative influence.

Indigo - This is the color of inertia; stops situations or people; best used in rituals that require a deep meditational state. Also stimulates Saturnian energy.

Ivory - (beige): neutrality, balance and harmlessness

Lavender - Mother consciousness, manifestation and selflessness, Spirituality, compassion, understanding, inspiration, make contact with Higher-Self, attract spiritual assistance, very calming.

Magenta - This is a combination of red and violet that oscillates on a high frequency. It's used to energize rituals where immediate action and high levels of power or spiritual healing are required.

Orange - Used as a balancing element, promotes mental agility, energy, success and stamina. It's used to affect legal matters, success, action and promotion. Gives encouragement, adaptability, stimulation, cleanses negative attitudes, situations and places.

Peach - Promotes restoration and rejuvenation, confers a softness and gentleness.

Pink - Represents emotions from the heart and raises energies. This is the standard for all rituals that are used to draw love.

Pink (Dark) - Represents friends and family, and healing in the family. Promotes romance, and friendship, brings hope. Can promote restful sleep.

Pink (Light) - Represents devotion, love, tenderness and faith. Feminine energy.

Purple - Is used to obtain desires, power and success. Can stimulate idealism and psychic manifestations and help make contact with the spiritual world, increases enthusiasm, desire and power. It is also powerful for healing, and spiritual development. Some attempt to use it for power over others.

Red - Represents physical pleasures. It can stimulate lust, courage, or strength against enemies. Can confer passion, love, and/or respect, stimulates energy, health, fertility and will power. It draws Aries and Scorpio energy. It increases magnetism in rituals. Also infers sex, vibrancy, and survival.

Rose - Rose is great for treating heart ailments, anxiety, and depression. Good for people who suffer from nightmares. This graceful color increases admiration, love, friendship, fidelity, and calmness. It can also arouse emotions. It stimulates compassion for self and others, higher mystical powers and humor.

Silver - Encourages stability; helps develop psychic abilities; attracts the influence of the Mother Goddess. Also can be used to stimulate mental telepathy, clairvoyance, and intuition. It can be used for cancellations and neutrality. It stimulates psychometry, dreams, female power, and astral energies/projection.

Turquoise - Is a color that can be used for healing, prosperity, peace, growth, awareness, meditation, creativity, neutrality and cancellation. Often used to represent the Goddess.

Violet - Strength, Success, Idealism, psychic revelation; Ideal for rituals which are designed to secure Ambition, Independence and financial success or to establish contact with the other, spiritual world; Enhances Neptune energy.

White - This has the highest consciousness to protect, purify, and heal. Represents truth, unity, protection, peace, purification, happiness, and spirituality. Some say it can be used to replace any color candle in rituals. Used for concentration rituals and meditation work. Lunar energy.

Yellow - Represents attraction, charm, confidence and persuasion. Used to stimulate mental clarity, knowledge and concentration. Also used in healing. Like gold, it can serve for magic and rituals involving solar energies and deities associated with the sun. Stimulates logic, aids in overcoming mental blocks and promoting the self.

Religions

A compiled list of religions from around the world.

Aladura - "Owners of Prayer", religious movement among the Yoruba peoples of western Nigeria, embracing some of the independent prophet-healing churches of West Africa. The movement, which in the early 1970s had several hundred thousand adherents, began about 1918 among the younger elite in the well-established Christian community. They were dissatisfied with Western religious forms and lack of spiritual power and were influenced by literature from the small U.S. divine-healing Faith Tabernacle Church of Philadelphia. The 1918 world influenza epidemic precipitated the formation of a prayer group of Anglican laymen at Ijebu-Ode, Nigeria; the group emphasized divine healing, prayer protection, and a puritanical moral code. By 1922 divergences from Anglican practice forced the separation of a group that became known as the Faith Tabernacle, with several small congregations.

Amish - are a group of traditionalist Christian church fellowships, closely related to but distinct from Mennonite churches, with which they share Swiss Anabaptist origins. The Amish are known for simple living, plain dress, and reluctance to adopt many conveniences of modern technology. The history of the Amish church began with a schism in Switzerland within a group of Swiss and Alsatian Anabaptists in 1693 led by Jakob Ammann. Those who followed Ammann became known as Amish.

Anglicanism - is a tradition within Christianity comprising the Church of England and churches which are historically tied to it or have similar beliefs, worship practices and church structures. The word Anglican originates in ecclesia anglicana, a Medieval Latin phrase dating to at least 1246 that means the English Church. Adherents of Anglicanism are called Anglicans. The great majority of Anglicans are members of churches which are part of the international Anglican Communion. There are, however, a number of churches outside of the Anglican Communion which also consider themselves to be Anglican, most notably those referred to as Continuing Anglican churches and those which are part of the Anglican realignment movement.

Asatru - is a form of Germanic Neopaganism which developed in the United States from the 1970s. It focuses on historical Norse paganism of the Viking

Age as described in the Eddas, but proponents also take a more inclusive approach, defining it as "Northern European Heathenry" not limited to a specific historical period.

Baha'i Faith - is a monotheistic religion emphasizing the spiritual unity of all humankind. Three core principles establish a basis for Baha'i teachings and doctrine: the unity of God, that there is only one God who is the source of all creation; the unity of religion, that all major religions have the same spiritual source and come from the same God; and the unity of humanity, that all humans have been created equal, and that diversity of race and culture are seen as worthy of appreciation and acceptance. According to the Baha'i Faith's teachings, the human purpose is to learn to know and love God through such methods as prayer, reflection and being of service to humanity.

Baptist - are individuals who comprise a group of denominations and churches that subscribe to a doctrine that baptism should be performed only for professing believers (believer's baptism, as opposed to infant baptism), and that it must be done by complete immersion (as opposed to effusion or sprinkling). Other tenets of Baptist churches include soul competency (liberty), salvation through faith alone, Scripture alone as the rule of faith and practice, and the autonomy of the local congregation. Baptists recognize two ministerial offices, pastors and deacons. Baptist churches are widely considered to be Protestant churches, though some Baptists disavow this identity. Diverse from their beginning, those identifying as Baptists today differ widely from one another in what they believe, how they worship, their attitudes toward other Christians, and their understanding of what is important in Christian discipleship.

Bon - is the term for the Tibetan religious tradition or sect, being distinct from Buddhist ones in its particular teachings and myths, although its terminology and rituals are largely (or partly) borrowed from Tibetan Buddhism. It arose in the eleventh century upward and established its scriptures mainly from terms and visions by tertöns such as Loden Nyingpo. Though Bon terma contain myths of Bon existing before the introduction of Buddhism in Tibet, "in truth the 'old religion' was a new religion.

Buddhism - is a nontheistic religion that encompasses a variety of traditions, beliefs and practices largely based on teachings attributed to Siddhartha Gautama, who is commonly known as the Buddha, meaning "the awakened one". According to Buddhist tradition, the Buddha lived and taught in the eastern part of the Indian subcontinent sometime between the 6th and 4th centuries BCE. He is recognized by Buddhists as an awakened or enlightened teacher who shared his insights to help sentient beings end their suffering through the elimination of ignorance and craving by way of understanding and the seeing of Dependent Origination and the Four Noble Truths, with the ultimate goal of attainment of the sublime state of Nirvana.

Candomble - is an African-Brazilian religion has around two million followers. It is a syncretic religion, meaning that it is a combination of various beliefs. At the core of the religion are the traditional African beliefs of Yoruba, Fon and Bantu. Candomble also has elements of Christianity, particularly of Catholicism. Candomble means "dance in honor of the gods." Accordingly, dance and music play important roles in the religion. At the center of Candomble is God or Oludumare. Deities called orixas serve Oludumare. Candomble does not have any holy scriptures.

Cao Dai - is a syncretist Vietnamese religious movement with a strongly nationalist political character. Cao Dai draws upon ethical precepts from Confucianism, occult practices from Taoism, theories of karma and rebirth from Buddhism, and a hierarchical organization (including a pope) from Roman Catholicism. Its pantheon of saints includes such diverse figures as the Buddha, Confucius, Jesus Christ, Muhammad, Pericles, Julius Caesar, Joan of Arc, Victor Hugo, and Sun Yat-sen.

Catholicism - is used as a broad term for describing specific traditions in the Christian churches in theology, doctrine, liturgy, ethics, and spirituality. In this sense, it is to be distinguished from the sense in which it denotes Christians and churches, western and eastern, that are in full communion with the Holy See, and that are commonly called the Catholic Church or Roman Catholic Church. In the sense of indicating historical continuity of faith and practice from the first millennium, the term "Catholicism" is at times employed to mark a contrast to Protestantism, which tends to look solely to the Bible as interpreted on the principles of the 16th-century Protestant Reformation as its ultimate standard. It was thus used by the Oxford movement.

Chinese Religion - China has long been a cradle and host to a variety of the most enduring religion-philosophical traditions of the world. Confucianism and Taoism, plus Buddhism, constitute the "three teachings", philosophical frameworks which historically have had a significant role in shaping Chinese culture. Elements of these three belief systems are often incorporated into the traditional folk religions. Chinese religions are family-oriented and do not demand exclusive adherence, allowing the practice or belief of several at the same time. Some scholars prefer not to use the term "religion" in reference to belief systems in China, and suggest "cultural practices", "thought systems" or "philosophies" as more appropriate terms. There is a stimulating debate over what to call religion and who should be called religious in China. The emperors of China claimed the Mandate of Heaven and participated in Chinese religious practices. Since 1949, China has been governed by the Communist Party of China, an atheist organization, which regulates the practice of religion in mainland China. It presently formally and institutionally recognizes five religions in China: Buddhism, Taoism, Islam, Protestantism, and Catholicism (though despite historic links, the Party enforces a separation of the Chinese Catholic Church from the Roman Catholic Church).

Chopra Center - founded in 1996 by Deepak Chopra, M.D. and David Simon, M.D., is the premier provider of experiences, education, teacher trainings and products that improve the health and wellbeing of body, mind and spirit. We provide an integrative approach to total wellbeing through self-awareness, and the practice of yoga, meditation and Ayurveda. The consciousness based teachings of Vedic science, as translated by our founders, coupled with cutting edge research and modern western medicine, serve as the foundation for Chopra Center teachings. We collaborate with visionaries, scientists, pioneers, physicians and industry experts to educate and inspire seekers from around the globe to better their lives and the lives of those around them.

Christianity - is an Abrahamic, monotheistic religion based on the life and oral teachings of Jesus of Nazareth as presented in the New Testament. Christianity is the world's largest religion, with approximately 2.2 billion adherents, known as Christians. Most Christians believe that Jesus is the Son of God, fully divine and fully human, and the savior of humanity whose coming was prophesied in the Old Testament. Consequently, Christians refer to Jesus as Christ or the Messiah.

Christian Science - is a set of beliefs and practices belonging to the metaphysical family of new religious movements. It was developed in 19th-century New England by Mary Baker Eddy (1821–1910), who argued in her book Science and Health (1875) that sickness is an illusion that can be corrected by prayer alone. The book became Christian Science's central text, along with the Bible, and by 2001 had sold ten million copies in 16 languages.

Confucianism - the ethical teachings formulated by Confucius and introduced into Chinese religion, emphasizing devotion to parents, family, and friends, cultivation of the mind, self-control, and just social activity.

Conservative Judaism - (also known as Masorti Judaism outside of the United States and Canada) is a modern stream of Ashkenazi Judaism that arose out of intellectual currents in Germany in the mid-19th century and took institutional form in the United States in the early 1900s.

Conservative Judaism has its roots in the school of thought known as Positive-Historical Judaism, developed in 1850s Germany as a reaction to the more liberal religious positions taken by Reform Judaism and put into practice from the 1840s in the Frankfurt and Berlin reform congregations. The term conservative was meant to signify that Jews should attempt to conserve Jewish tradition, rather than reform or abandon it, and does not imply the movement's adherents are politically conservative. In many countries outside the United States and Canada, including Israel and the UK, it is today known as Masorti Judaism (Hebrew for "Traditional").

Divine Science - is a religious movement within the wider New Thought movement. The group was formalized in San Francisco in the 1880s under Malinda Cramer. "In March 1888 Cramer and her husband Frank chartered the 'Home College of Spiritual Science.' Two months later Cramer changed the name of her school to the 'Home College of Divine Science, during the dramatic growth of the New Thought Movement in the United States.

Eckankar - is a religious movement founded by Paul Twitchell in 1965. The personal experience of the "Light and Sound of God" is one of the aims of the many spiritual exercises that are delineated in the numerous books available to the general public as well as in the discourses accessible to members only. Eckankar followers believe it provides an individual spiritual path to an understanding of self as eternal Soul and the development of higher states of consciousness. Followers of Eckankar commonly refer to themselves as "Eckists".

Epicureanism - is a system of philosophy based upon the teachings of the ancient Greek philosopher Epicurus, founded around 307 BC. Epicurus was an atomic materialist, following in the steps of Democritus. His materialism led him to a general attack on superstition and divine intervention. Following Aristippus—about whom very little is known—Epicurus believed that what he called "pleasure" is the greatest good, but the way to attain such pleasure is to live modestly and to gain knowledge of the workings of the world and the limits of one's desires. This led one to attain a state of tranquility (ataraxia) and freedom from fear, as well as absence of bodily pain (aponia). The combination of these two states is supposed to constitute happiness in its highest form. Although Epicureanism is a form of hedonism, insofar as it declares pleasure to be the sole intrinsic good, its conception of absence of pain as the greatest pleasure and its advocacy of a simple life make it different from "hedonism" as it is commonly understood.

Episcopalianism - An episcopal church has bishops in its organizational structure which is called Episcopal polity.

Falun Gong - is a Chinese spiritual discipline that combines meditation and qigong exercises with a moral philosophy centered on the tenets of Truthfulness, Compassion, and Forbearance. The practice emphasizes morality and the cultivation of virtue, and identifies as a qigong practice of the Buddhist school, though its teachings also incorporate elements drawn from Taoist traditions. Through moral rectitude and the practice of meditation, practitioners of Falun Gong aspire to better health and, ultimately, spiritual enlightenment.

Germanic Heathenism - also known as Heathenry, Ásatrú, Odinism, Forn Siðr, Wotanism, Theodism, and other names, is the contemporary revival of historical polytheistic Germanic paganism. Dedicated to the ancient gods and goddesses of the North, the focus of Germanic Neopaganism varies considerably, from strictly historical polytheistic reconstructionism to syncretist (eclectic), Jungian, occult or mysticist approaches. Germanic neopagan organizations cover a wide spectrum of belief and ideals. Much of Germanic Neopaganism's origins are in 19th century romanticism, as the aboriginal cultures of Northern Europe came to be glorified. In the early 20th century, organized groups emerged in Germany and Austria. In the 1970s, new Germanic Neopagan organizations grew up in Europe and North America, although a broad division in the movement emerged between the folkish movement, who saw it as the indigenous religion of the Nordic peoples, and the universalist movement, who opposed strictly racialist interpretations. As present, established Germanic Pagan communities exist in Europe, North America, South America, and Australasia. A few adherents can even be found in South Africa.

Germanic paganism - refers to the theology and religious practices of the Germanic peoples from the Iron Age until their Christianization during the Medieval period. It has been described as being "a system of interlocking and closely interrelated religious worldviews and practices rather than as one indivisible religion" and as such consisted of "individual worshippers, family traditions and regional cults within a broadly consistent framework". Germanic paganism took various forms in different areas of the Germanic world. The best documented version was that of 10th and 11th century Norse religion, although other information can be found from Anglo-Saxon and Continental Germanic sources. Scattered references are also found in the earliest writings of other Germanic peoples and Roman descriptions. The information can be supplemented with archaeological finds and remnants of pre-Christian beliefs in later folklore.

Greco-Roman Religion - is an umbrella term used to refer to many religious traditions practiced within the Roman Empire and eventually syncretized and assimilated into something resembling a complex whole. It originated largely in the pre-existing mythology of ancient Greece, which was appropriated by the Romans into their own religious practices. In its latter years, when it competed with Christianity, it was referred to by followers of that religion as paganism.

Hare Krishna (ISKCON) - known colloquially as the Hare Krishna movement or Hare Krishna's, is a Gaudiya Vaishnava religious organization. It was founded in 1966 in New York City by A. C. Bhakti Vedanta Swami Prabhupada. Its core beliefs are based on select traditional Hindu scriptures, particularly the Bhagavad-gītā and the Śrīmad Bhāgavatam. ISKCON is an authorized branch that claims to be a direct descendant of Brahma-Madhva-Gaudiya Vaishnava Sampradaya. The appearance of the movement and its culture come from the Gaudiya Vaishnava tradition, which has had adherents in India since the late

15th century and Western converts since the early 1900s in America, and in England in the 1930s.

ISKCON was formed to spread the practice of bhakti yoga, in which those involved (bhaktas) dedicate their thoughts and actions towards pleasing the Supreme Lord, Krishna. ISKCON today is a worldwide confederation of more than 550 centers, including 60 farm communities, some aiming for self-sufficiency, 50 schools and 90 restaurants. In recent decades the movement's most rapid expansions in terms of numbers of membership have been within Eastern Europe (especially since the collapse of the Soviet Union) and India.

Hasidic Judaism - is a branch of Orthodox Judaism that promotes spirituality through the popularization and internalization of Jewish mysticism as the fundamental aspect of the faith. It was founded in 18th-century Eastern Europe by Rabbi Israel Baal Shem Tov as a reaction against overly legalistic Judaism. His example began the characteristic veneration of leadership in Hasidism as embodiments and intercessors of Divinity for the followers. Contrary to this, Hasidic teachings cherished the sincerity and concealed holiness of the unlettered common folk, and their equality with the scholarly elite. The emphasis on the Immanent Divine presence in everything gave new value to prayer and deeds of kindness, alongside rabbinical supremacy of study, and replaced historical mystical (Kabbalistic) and ethical (musar) asceticism and admonishment with Simcha, encouragement, and daily fervor. This populist emotional revival accompanied the elite ideal of nullification to paradoxical Divine Panentheism, through intellectual articulation of inner dimensions of mystical thought.

Hellenic Reconstructionism - The Hellenic religion is a traditional religion and way of life, revolving around the Greek Gods, primarily focused on the Twelve Olympians, and embracing ancient Hellenic values and virtues.

Hinduism - is the dominant religion of the Indian subcontinent, and consists of many diverse traditions. It includes Shaivism, Vaishnavism and Shaktism among numerous other traditions, and a wide spectrum of laws and prescriptions of "daily morality" based on karma, dharma, and societal norms. Hinduism is a categorization of distinct intellectual or philosophical points of view, rather than a rigid, common set of beliefs. Hinduism has been called the "oldest religion" in the world, and some practitioners refer to it as Sanatana Dharma, "the eternal law" or the "eternal way" beyond human origins. It prescribes the "eternal" duties all Hindus have to follow, regardless of class, caste, or sect, such as honesty, purity, and self-restraint.

Islam - is a monotheistic and Abrahamic religion articulated by the Qur'an, a book considered by its adherents to be the verbatim word of God and by the teachings and normative example (called the Sunnah and composed of hadith) of Muhammad, considered by them to be the last prophet of God. An adherent of Islam is called a Muslim.

Jainism - traditionally known as Jaina Shasana or Jaina dharma is a nontheistic Indian religion that prescribes a path of ahimsa - nonviolence - towards all living beings, and emphasizes spiritual independence and equality between all forms of life. Practitioners believe that nonviolence and self-control are the means by which they can obtain liberation. Currently Jainism is divided into two major sects, Śvētāmbara and Digambara.

Jehovah's Witnesses - is a millenarian restorationist Christian denomination with nontrinitarian beliefs distinct from mainstream Christianity. According to August 2013 organizational statistics published in the 2014 Yearbook of Jehovah's Witnesses, worldwide membership exceeded 7.9 million adherents involved in evangelism, convention attendance exceeded 14 million, and annual Memorial attendance exceeded 19.2 million. Jehovah's Witnesses are directed by the Governing Body of Jehovah's Witnesses, a group of elders in Brooklyn, New York, which establishes all doctrines based on its interpretations of the Bible; they prefer to use their own translation, the New World Translation of the Holy Scriptures. They believe that the destruction of the present world system at Armageddon is imminent, and that the establishment of God's kingdom on earth is the only solution for all problems faced by humanity.

Judaism - is the religion, philosophy, and way of life of the Jewish people. Judaism is a monotheistic religion, with the Torah as its foundational text and supplemental oral tradition represented by later texts such as the Midrash and the Talmud. Judaism is considered by religious Jews to be the expression of the covenantal relationship that God established with the Children of Israel.

Kemetic Reconstructionism - is the contemporary revival of Ancient Egyptian religion emerging from the 1970s onwards. Followers call themselves Kemetic. Also known as Egyptian Neopaganism, the religion has an organized presence in the United States, France and the Czech Republic. There are several main groups, each of which takes a different approach to their beliefs, ranging from eclectic to reconstructionistic. However, all of these can be identified as belonging to three strains: traditional "Orthodox" Kemetism (adopting a philological approach, also Kemetic Orthodoxy), Black Kemetism (emerged amongst black people in the United States and France, and related to afrocentric ideologies), and Neo-Atenism.

Lutheranism - is a major branch of Western Christianity that identifies with the theology of Martin Luther, a German monk and theologian. Luther's efforts to reform the theology and practice of the Roman Catholic Church launched the Protestant Reformation in German-speaking territories of the Holy Roman Empire. Beginning with the 95 Theses, first published in 1517, Luther's writings were disseminated internationally, spreading the early ideas of the Reformation beyond the influence and control of the Roman Catholic Curia and the Holy Roman Emperor. The split between the Lutherans and the Roman Catholics was made clear and open with the 1521 Edict of Worms: the edicts of the Diet condemned Luther and officially outlawed citizens of the Holy Roman Empire from defending or propagating his ideas, subjecting advocates of Lutheranism to forfeiture of all property, specifying half of any seized property forfeit to the Imperial government and the remaining half forfeit to the party who brought the accusation. The divide primarily centered over the doctrine of Justification.

Mahayana Buddhism - is one of the three main existing branches of Buddhism and a term for classification of Buddhist philosophies and practice. According to the teachings of Mahāyāna traditions, "Mahāyāna" also refers to the path of the Bodhisattva seeking complete enlightenment for the benefit of all sentient beings, also called "Bodhisattva Yana", or the "Bodhisattva Vehicle." A bodhisattva who has accomplished this goal is called a samyaksaṃbuddha, or "fully enlightened Buddha." A samyaksaṃbuddha can establish the Dharma and lead disciples to enlightenment.

Mayan Religion - The traditional Maya religion of Guatemala, Belize, western Honduras, and the Tabasco, Chiapas, and Yucatán regions of Mexico is a southeastern variant of Mesoamerican religion. As is the case with many other contemporary Mesoamerican religions, it results from centuries of symbiosis with Roman Catholicism. When its pre-Spanish antecedents are taken into account, however, traditional Maya religion already exists for more than two millennia as a recognizably distinct phenomenon. Before the advent of Christianity, it was spread over many indigenous kingdoms, all with their own local traditions. Today, it coexists and interacts with pan-Mayan syncretism, the're-invention of tradition' by the Pan-Maya movement, and Christianity in its various denominations.

Mithraism - were a mystery religion practiced in the Roman Empire from about the 1st to 4th centuries AD. The name of the Persian god Mithra (proto-Indo-Iranian Mitra), adapted into Greek as Mithras, was linked to a new and distinctive imagery. Writers of the Roman Empire period referred to this mystery religion by phrases which can be anglicized as Mysteries of Mithras or Mysteries of the Persians; modern historians refer to it as Mithraism, or sometimes Roman Mithraism. The mysteries were popular in the Roman military.

Mormonism (LDS) - is the predominant religious tradition of the Latter Day Saint movement of Restorationist Christianity. This movement was founded by Joseph Smith, Jr., in the 1820s. During the 1830s and 1840s, Mormonism gradually distinguished itself from traditional Protestantism. Mormonism today represents the new, non-Protestant faith taught by Smith in the 1840s. After Smith's death, most Mormons followed Brigham Young west, calling themselves The Church of Jesus Christ of Latter-day Saints (LDS Church). Other variations of Mormonism include Mormon fundamentalism, which seeks to maintain practices and doctrines such as polygamy that were abandoned by the LDS Church, and various other small independent denominations.

Neopaganism - also known as contemporary paganism, and Neopaganism, is a group of contemporary religious movements influenced by or claiming to be derived from the various historical pagan beliefs of pre-modern Europe. Although they do share commonalities, contemporary Pagan religious movements are diverse and no single set of beliefs, practices, or texts are shared by them all. "Contemporary Paganism" as practiced in the United States in the 1990s has been described as "a synthesis of historical inspiration and present-day creativity", Adherents rely on pre-Christian, folkloric and ethnographic sources to a variety of degrees; many follow a spirituality which they accept is entirely modern, whilst others attempt to reconstruct or revive indigenous, ethnic religions as found in historical and folkloric sources as accurately as possible. Polytheism, animism, and pantheism are common features in Pagan theology.

New Thought - is a spiritual movement, sometimes classed as a Christian denomination, which developed in the United States in the 19th century, following the teachings of Phineas Quimby. The three major organizations within New Thought movement today are Religious Science, Unity Church and the Church of Divine Science, with an estimated number of some 1,500,000 adherents in the United States between them. There are numerous smaller groups, most of which are incorporated in the International New Thought Alliance.

Nichiren Buddhism - is a branch of Buddhism based on the teachings of the 13th century Japanese monk Nichiren (1222–1282). Nichiren Buddhism is generally noted for its focus on the Lotus Sutra and an attendant belief that all people have an innate Buddha nature and are therefore inherently capable of attaining enlightenment in their current form and present lifetime. It is also notable for its hard-liner opposition to any other form of Buddhism, which Nichiren saw as deviating from the Buddhist truth he had discovered. Nichiren Buddhism is a comprehensive term covering several major schools and many sub-schools, as well as several of Japan's new religions. Its many denominations have in common a strong focus on the chanting and recital of the Lotus Sutra, which is thought to hold "extraordinary power".

Occult - is "knowledge of the hidden". In common English usage, occult refers to "knowledge of the paranormal", as opposed to "knowledge of the measurable", usually referred to as science. The term is sometimes taken to mean knowledge that "is meant only for certain people" or that "must be kept hidden", but for most practicing occultists it is simply the study of a deeper spiritual reality that extends beyond pure reason and the physical sciences. The terms esoteric and arcane have very similar meanings, and in most contexts the three terms are interchangeable. It also describes a number of magical organizations or orders, the teachings and practices taught by them, and to a large body of current and historical literature and spiritual philosophy related to this subject.

Orthodox Christianity - is a collective term for the Eastern Orthodox Church and Oriental Orthodoxy. Each of these two branches of Christianity uses the term "orthodoxy" (from Greek: orthos + doxa, meaning correct belief) to express its belief that it has an unbroken connection to the faith, doctrine and practices of the ancient Christian church. The adjectives "Eastern" and "Oriental" are used by outsiders to differentiate the two groups; the adherents of each group call their own group simply "Orthodox Christians". The two groups have been divided by their disagreements over the nature of Christ since the 5th century, and they are currently not in communion with each other, but they maintain many identical doctrines, similar Church structures, and similar worship practices. There have been a number of recent talks aimed at reunification, and a great deal of agreement has been reached, but no concrete steps have been taken towards formal unity as yet.

Orthodox Judaism - is the approach to religious Judaism which adheres to the interpretation and application of the laws and ethics of the Torah as legislated in the Talmudic texts by the Tanaim and Amoraim and subsequently developed and applied by the later authorities known as the Gaonim, Rishonim, and Acharonim. Orthodox Judaism generally includes Modern Orthodox Judaism and ultra-orthodox or Haredi Judaism, but complete within is a wide range of philosophies. Orthodox Judaism is a modern self-conscious identification that, for some, distinguishes it from traditional premodern Judaism, although it was the mainstream expression of Judaism prior to the 19th century.

Presbyterianism - is a branch of Reformed Protestantism which traces its origins to the British Isles. Presbyterian churches derive their name from the Presbyterian form of church government, which is government by representative assemblies of elders. Many Reformed churches are organized this way, but the word "Presbyterian," when capitalized, is often applied uniquely to the churches that trace their roots to the Scottish and English churches that bore that name and English political groups that formed during the English Civil War. Presbyterian theology typically emphasizes the sovereignty of God, the authority of the Scriptures, and the necessity of grace through faith in Christ. Presbyterian church government was ensured in Scotland by the Acts of Union in 1707 which created the kingdom of Great Britain. In fact, most Presbyterians found in England can trace a Scottish connection, and the Presbyterian denomination was also taken to North America mostly by Scots and Scots-Irish (Scotch-Irish American) immigrants. The Presbyterian denominations in Scotland hold to the theology of John Calvin and his immediate successors, although there is a range of theological views within contemporary Presbyterianism.

Protestantism - is the form of Christian faith and practice that originated with the Protestant Reformation. The Reformation was a movement against what Protestants considered to be the errors of the Roman Catholic Church. It is one of the largest divisions of Christianity; along with Catholicism and Eastern Orthodoxy. The term refers to the letter of protestation by Lutheran princes in 1529 against an edict condemning the teachings of Martin Luther as heresy.

Pure Land Buddhism - in English, is a broad branch of Mahāyāna Buddhism and one of the most widely practiced traditions of Buddhism in East Asia. Pure Land is a tradition of Buddhist teachings that are focused on Amitabh Buddha.

Quakers - are members of a family of religious movements collectively known as the Religious Society of Friends. The central unifying doctrine of these movements is the priesthood of all believers, a doctrine derived from a verse in the New Testament, 1 Peter 2:9. Most Friends view themselves as members of a Christian denomination. They include those with evangelical, holiness, liberal, and traditional conservative Quaker understandings of Christianity. Unlike many other groups that emerged within Christianity, the Religious Society of Friends has actively tried to avoid creeds and hierarchical structures. In 2007 there were approximately 359,000 adult members of Quaker meetings in the world.

Rastafari - is an Ethiopian-Hebrew spirituality that arose in the 1930s in the Americas and became popular in Jamaica. It is sometimes described as a religion but is considered by many adherents to be a "Way of Life". Its adherents worship Haile Selassie I, Emperor of Ethiopia (ruled 1930–1974), some as Jesus in his Second Advent, or as God the Father. Members of the Rastafari way of life are known as Rastas, or the Rastafari. The way of life is sometimes referred to as "Rastafarianism", but this term is considered derogatory and offensive by most Rastafari, who, being highly critical of "isms" (which they see as a typical part of "Babylon culture"); dislike being labelled as an "ism" themselves.

Religious Science - was established in 1927 by Ernest Holmes (1887–1960) and is a spiritual, philosophical and metaphysical religious movement within the New Thought movement. In general, the term "Science of Mind" applies to the teachings, while the term "Religious Science" applies to the organizations. However, adherents often use the terms interchangeably.

Satanism - is a broad group of social movements comprising diverse ideological and philosophical beliefs. Their shared features include symbolic association with or admiration for Satan, who Satanists see as a liberating figure. It was estimated that there were 50,000 Satanists in 1990. There may be as many as one hundred thousand Satanists in the world. Particularly after the European Enlightenment, some works, such as Paradise Lost, were taken up by Romantics and described as presenting the biblical Satan as an allegory representing a crisis of faith, individualism, free will, wisdom and enlightenment. Those works actually featuring Satan as a heroic character are fewer in number, but do exist; George Bernard Shaw, and Mark Twain included such characterizations in their works long before religious Satanists took up the pen. From then on, Satan and Satanism started to gain a new meaning outside of Christianity. Although the public practice of Satanism began with the founding of The Church of Satan in 1966, historical precedents exist: a group called the Ophite Cultus Satanas was founded in Ohio by Herbert Arthur Sloane in 1948. Satanist groups that appeared after the 1960s are widely diverse, but two major trends are theistic Satanism and atheistic Satanism. Theistic Satanists venerate Satan as a supernatural deity, viewing him not as omnipotent but rather as a patriarch. In contrast, atheistic Satanists regard Satan as merely a symbol of certain human traits.

Scientology - is a body of beliefs and related practices created by science fiction writer L. Ron Hubbard (1911–1986), beginning in 1952 as a successor to his earlier self-help system, Dianetics. Hubbard characterized Scientology as a religion, and in 1953 he incorporated the Church of Scientology in Camden, New Jersey. Scientology teaches that people are immortal beings who have forgotten their true nature. Its method of spiritual rehabilitation is a type of counselling known as auditing, in which practitioners aim to consciously re-experience painful or traumatic events in their past in order to free themselves of their limiting effects. Study materials and auditing sessions are made available to members on a fee-for-service basis, which the church describes as a "fixed donation". Scientology is legally recognized as a tax-exempt religion in the United States, Italy, South Africa, Australia, Sweden, the Netherlands, New Zealand, Portugal, and Spain the Church of Scientology emphasizes this as proof that it is a bona fide religion. In contrast, the organization is considered a commercial enterprise in Switzerland, a cult (secte) in France and Chile, and a non-profit in Norway and its legal classification is often a point of contention.

Seventh-day Adventist - is a Protestant Christian denomination distinguished by its observance of Saturday, the original seventh day of the Judeo-Christian week, as the Sabbath, and by its emphasis on the imminent second coming (advent) of Jesus Christ. The denomination grew out of the Millerite movement in the United States during the middle part of the 19th century and was formally established in 1863. Among its founders was Ellen G. White, whose extensive writings are still held in high regard by the church today.

Shaivism - is one of the four most widely followed sects of Hinduism, which reveres the god Shiva as the Supreme Being. It is also known as śaiva paṁtha, they believe that Shiva is All and in all, the creator, preserver, destroyer, revealer and concealer of all that is. Shaivism is widespread throughout India, Nepal and Sri Lanka. Areas notable for the practice of Shaivism include parts of Southeast Asia, especially Malaysia, Singapore, and Indonesia.

Shamanism - is a practice that involves a practitioner reaching altered states of consciousness in order to encounter and interact with the spirit world and channel these transcendental energies into this world. A shaman is a person regarded as having access to, and influence in, the world of benevolent and malevolent spirits, who typically enters into a trance state during a ritual, and practices divination and healing.

Shinto - is the indigenous religion of Japan and the people of Japan. It is defined as an action-centered religion, focused on ritual practices to be carried out diligently, to establish a connection between present-day Japan and its ancient past. Founded in 660 BC according to Japanese mythology, Shinto practices were first recorded and codified in the written historical records of the Kojiki and Nihon Shoki in the 8th century. Still, these earliest Japanese writings do not refer to a unified "Shinto religion", but rather to a collection of native beliefs and mythology. Shinto today is a term that applies to the religion of public shrines devoted to the worship of a multitude of gods (kami), suited to various purposes such as war memorials and harvest festivals, and applies as well to various sectarian organizations. Practitioners express their diverse beliefs through a standard language and practice, adopting a similar style in dress and ritual, dating from around the time of the Nara and Heian periods.

Sikhism - is a monotheistic religion founded during the 15th century in the Punjab region of the Indian subcontinent by Guru Nanak and developed through the teachings of ten successive Sikh Gurus (the eleventh and last Guru being the holy scripture Guru Granth Sahib: a collection of the Sikh Gurus' writings that was first compiled by the fifth Sikh Guru). It is the fifth-largest organized religion in the world, with approximately 30 million adherents. Punjab, India, is the only state in the world with a majority Sikh population.

Stoicism - is a school of Hellenistic philosophy founded in Athens by Zeno of Citium in the early 3rd century BC. The Stoics taught that destructive emotions resulted from errors in judgment, and that a sage, or person of "moral and intellectual perfection", would not suffer such emotions. Stoics were concerned with the active relationship between cosmic determinism and human freedom, and the belief that it is virtuous to maintain a will (called prohairesis) that is in accord with nature. Because of this, the Stoics presented their philosophy as a way of life, and they thought that the best indication of an individual's philosophy was not what a person said but how that person behaved.

Tendai Buddhism - is a Japanese school of Mahayana Buddhism, a descendant of the Chinese Tiantai or Lotus Sutra school. Although Tendai has the reputation of being a major denomination in Japanese history, and the most comprehensive and diversified school of Chinese Buddhism, it is almost unknown in the West. This meagre presence is in marked contrast to the vision of the founder of the movement in China, T'ien-t'ai Chih-i (538-597), who provided a religious framework which seemed suited to adapt to other cultures, to evolve new practices, and to universalize Buddhism.

Theravada Buddhism - is the oldest surviving branch of Buddhism. The name Theravada literally means "the Teaching of the Elders." It is relatively conservative, and according to Rupert Gethin, it is closer to early Buddhism than other existing Buddhist traditions.

Taoism - is a philosophical, ethical, and religious tradition of Chinese origin that emphasizes living in harmony with the Tao (also Romanized as Dao). The term Tao means "way", "path" or "principle", and can also be found in Chinese philosophies and religions other than Taoism. In Taoism, however, Tao denotes something that is both the source and the driving force behind everything that exists.

Tibetan Buddhism - is the body of Buddhist religious doctrine and institutions characteristic of Tibet, Mongolia, Tuva, Bhutan, Kalmykia and certain regions of the Himalayas, including northern Nepal, and India (particularly in Arunachal Pradesh, Ladakh, Dharamsala, Lahaul and Spiti in Himachal Pradesh, and Sikkim). It is the state religion of Bhutan. It is also practiced in Mongolia and parts of Russia (Kalmykia, Buryatia, and Tuva) and Northeast China. Texts recognized as scripture and commentaries are contained in the Tibetan Buddhist canon, such that Tibetan is a spiritual language of these areas.

Umbanda - is a Brazilian religion that blends African religions with Catholicism, Spiritism, and considerable indigenous lore. Umbanda is related to, and has many similarities with, other Afro-Brazilian religions like Candomblé and Quimbanda, but has its own identity. Although some of its beliefs and most of its practices existed in the late 19th century in almost all Brazil, it is assumed that Umbanda originated in Rio de Janeiro and surrounding areas in the early 20th century, mainly due to the work of a psychic (medium), Zélio Fernandino de Moraes, who practiced Umbanda among the poor Afro-Brazilian population. Since then, Umbanda has spread across mainly southern Brazil and neighboring countries like Uruguay and Argentina.

Unification Church - founded as the Holy Spirit Association for the Unification of World Christianity, and commonly called the Unification Church or Unificationism, is a new religious movement founded in South Korea in 1954 by Sun Myung Moon. Since its founding, the church has expanded throughout the world with most members living in East Asia.

Unitarian Universalism - is a liberal religion characterized by a "free and responsible search for truth and meaning". Unitarian Universalists do not share a creed but are unified by their shared search for spiritual growth. The roots of Unitarian Universalism are in liberal Christianity, specifically Unitarianism and Universalism. From these traditions comes a deep regard for intellectual freedom and inclusive love, so that congregations and members seek inspiration and derive spiritual practices from all major world religions.

Unity Church - is a spiritual philosophical movement within the wider New Thought movement and is best known to many through its Daily Word devotional publication. It describes itself as a "positive, practical Christianity" which "teach the effective daily application of the principles of Truth taught and exemplified by Jesus Christ" and promotes "a way of life that leads to health, prosperity, happiness, and peace of mind.

Vampirism - is an alternative lifestyle, based on the modern perception of vampires in popular fiction. The vampire subculture has stemmed largely from the Goth subculture, but also incorporates some elements of the sadomasochism subculture. The Internet provides a prevalent forum for the subculture along with other media such as glossy magazines devoted to the topic. Many self-professed vampires actively resent the term "lifestyles," as this tends to carry the connotation that vampirism is not real. Some vampires actually use the term as a pejorative for role-players. Active vampirism within the vampire subculture includes both sanguinarian vampirism, which involves blood consumption, and psychic vampirism, whose practitioners believe they are drawing spiritual nourishment from auric or pranic energy.

Vaishnavism - is one of the major branches of Hinduism along with Shaivism, Smartism, and Shaktism. It is focused on the veneration of Vishnu. Vaishnavites, or the followers of the Vishnu, lead a way of life promoting differentiated monotheism (henotheism), which gives importance to Vishnu and his ten incarnations. Followers worship Vishnu, the preserver god of the Hindu Trimurti ('three images', the Trinity), and his ten incarnations, including Rama and Krishna. The adherents of this sect are generally non-ascetic, monastic and devoted to meditative practice and ecstatic chanting. Vaishnavites are mainly dualistic. They are deeply devotional. Their religion is rich in saints, temples and scriptures.

Voodoo - is related to the religion of the West Indies associated with charms, fetishes and sorcery, or a religion based on beliefs and practices of African and Roman Catholic origin.

Westboro Baptist Church - is an American unaffiliated Baptist church known for its extreme ideologies, especially those against gay people. The church is widely described as a hate group and is monitored as such by the Anti-Defamation League and Southern Poverty Law Center. It was headed by Fred Phelps (although shortly before his death in March 2014, church representatives said that the church had not had a defined leader in "a very long time"), and consists primarily of members of his extended family; in 2011, the church stated that it had about 40 members. The church is headquartered in a residential neighborhood on the west side of Topeka about three miles (5 km) west of the Kansas State Capitol. Its first public service was held on the afternoon of November 27, 1955.

Wicca - is a modern pagan, witchcraft religion. It was developed in England during the first half of the 20th century and it was introduced to the public in 1954 by Gerald Gardner, a retired British civil servant. It draws upon a diverse set of ancient pagan and 20th century hermetic motifs for its theological structure and ritual practice. Wicca is a diverse religion with no central authority or figure defining it. It is divided into various lineages and denominations, referred to as traditions, each with its own organizational structure and level of centralization. Due to its decentralized nature, there is some disagreement over what actually constitutes Wicca. Some traditions, collectively referred to as British Traditional Wicca, strictly follow the initiatory lineage of Gardner and consider the term Wicca to apply only to such lineage traditions, while other eclectic traditions do not. Wicca is typically duo theistic, worshipping a god and goddess traditionally viewed as a mother goddess and horned god. These two deities are sometimes viewed as facets of a greater pantheistic godhead. However, beliefs range from hard polytheism to even monotheism. Wiccan celebration follows approximately eight seasonally based festivals known as Sabbaths. An unattributed statement known as the Wiccan Rede is the traditional basis of Wiccan morality. Wicca often involves the ritual practice of magic, though it is not always necessary.

Witchcraft - broadly means the practice of, and belief in, magical skills and abilities that are able to be exercised individually, by designated social groups, or by persons with the necessary esoteric secret knowledge. Witchcraft is a complex concept that varies culturally and societally, therefore it is difficult to define with precision and cross-cultural assumptions about the meaning or significance of the term should be applied with caution. Witchcraft often occupies a religious, divinatory, or medicinal role, and is often present within societies and groups whose cultural framework includes a magical world view. Although witchcraft can often share common ground with related concepts such as sorcery, the paranormal, magic, superstition, necromancy, possession, shamanism, healing, spiritualism, nature worship, and the occult, it is usually seen as distinct from these when examined by sociologists and anthropologists. The concept of witchcraft and the belief in its existence has existed since the dawn of human history. It has been present or central at various times, and in many diverse forms, among cultures and religions worldwide, including both "primitive" and "highly advanced" cultures, and continues to have an important role in many cultures today. Scientifically, the existence of magical powers and witchcraft are generally believed to lack credence and to be unsupported by high quality experimental testing, although individual witchcraft practices and effects may be open to scientific explanation or explained via mentalism and psychology.

Worldwide Church of God - is an evangelical Christian denomination based in Glendora, California, United States. Founded in 1934 by Herbert W. Armstrong as a religious broadcasting radio ministry named Radio Church of God, the Worldwide Church of God had a significant, and often controversial, influence on 20th-century religious broadcasting and publishing in the United States and Europe, especially in the field of interpreting biblical end-time prophecies. Within a few years after Armstrong's death in 1986, the succeeding church administration modified the denomination's doctrines and teachings to be compatible with mainstream evangelical Christianity, while many members and ministers left and formed other churches that conformed too many, but not all, of Armstrong's teachings. In 2009, the church adopted its current name.

Zen - is a school of Mahayana Buddhism that developed in China during the 6th century as Chan. From China, Zen spread south to Vietnam, northeast to Korea and east to Japan.

Zoroastrianism - is an ancient Iranian religion and a religious philosophy. It was once the state religion of the Achaemenid, Parthian, and Sasanian empires. Estimates of the current number of Zoroastrians worldwide vary between 145,000 and 2.6 million.

Spiritual Protection

An old saying tells us that where there is good, there is bad. Where there is light, there is darkness. Where there are angels, there are demons. Paranormal phenomenon are no exception. When investigating buildings, homes, outdoor sites we cannot be sure which we might encounter, so we must prepare for the worst and hope for the best. While most often activity is positive or neutral, there is always the possibility of encountering a negative spirit, or on rare occasions a demon. Many teams and individual researchers choose from an array of methods to protect themselves before, and sometimes during and after an investigation.

In order to ward off negative or demonic entities, protection prayers are recited. These prayers are not necessarily considered to remove demons that are already present. Instead, they are meant to prevent demonic entities from entering, or otherwise influencing a person, family, home, property, or object. The type of prayer is a decision of the person, investigator or team, based on their belief system.

Spiritual Prayers of Protection

"I seek protection and sound my alarm, my body, mind and spirit be safe from harm. My aura a shield to help me stay strong, I block negativity and all that is wrong"

"Great Divine spirit, I ask for your guidance and protection at this time. May all who come forward be of and from the light. I ask my guardian spirit to block all negative entities or spirits from being present in this place. And so it is"

"In the name of all that is goodness and light, surround our circle in the white light of holy protection. We ask that no harm befalls or follows the protected circle and that our quest benefit all who are among us. In the name of all that

is goodness and light, we thank thee for your protection of holy white light.
Amen"

"Great Spirits, Creators of All That Is, Please send to me the most positive
energy and light possible in this time and space to watch over me and those I
share this experience with. Send to us the highest force or forces possible to
keep us safe, focused and positive in our intent. In return we give thanks and
gratitude, love and positive light for the universal good of all. Blessings be
upon us"

"Lord, make me an instrument of your peace. Where there is hatred, let me
sow love; where there is injury, pardon; where there is doubt, faith, where
there is despair, hope, where there is darkness, light, where there is sadness,
joy. O, Divine Master, grant that I may not so much seek to be consoled as to
console, to be understood as to understand, to be loved as to love, For it is in
giving that we receive, it is in pardoning that we are pardoned, it is in dying
that we are born again to eternal life."

The Lord's Prayer

Our Father, who art in heaven,
hallowed be thy Name,
thy kingdom come,
thy will be done,
on earth as it is in heaven.

Give us this day our daily bread.
And forgive us our trespasses,
as we forgive those
who trespass against us.

And lead us not into temptation,
but deliver us from evil.

For thine is the kingdom,
and the power, and the glory,
forever and ever. Amen.

The Prayer to the Archangel Michael

"Saint Michael the Archangel, Defend us in battle. Be our protection against the wickedness and snares of the Devil. May God rebuke him, we humbly pray. And do thou, O Prince of the heavenly host, by the power of God, thrust into hell Satan and all evil spirits. Who wander through the world for the ruin of souls. Amen"

Basic Protection and Calming Chant

"I am peaceful, I am strong and I am calm. The Goddess protects me from all harm. I am surrounded by her arms"

Spell of Protection

"On this night, I invoke the powers of fire to protect me from all that would harm me, whether physically, mentally, emotionally or spiritually"

"Great Goddess of day and night Protect me with all your might"

"In this place and in this hour By the guardians of the secrets of the night Take the keys to my heart And close the doors of my mind"

"The breath of life and the light of my mind creates an enchantment of protection and comfort as the air I breathe is purified, I surround myself with an orb of gold, this golden haze is constantly purified and separated from any negativity. May my space be protected."

For A Home

"Goddess of the hearth, beat strong and pure in the heart of my home. Lord of the threshold, keep vigilant guard over the entrance to my home. Spirits of the land, keep watch throughout the yard of my home. God of the borders, stand ready to repulse all disorder from my home."

For A Family

"Visit, O Lord, my home and all my family, and drive far from them all snares of the enemy. Let Thy holy angels dwell in it to preserve us in peace, and may Thy Blessing be upon us evermore; through Jesus Christ our Lord. Amen."

Guardian Angel Prayer

"Angel of God, guardian dear, to whom God's love commits me here, ever this day be at my side, to light, to guard to rule and guide. Amen."

Light Of God

"The Light of God surrounds me, The Love of God enfolds me, The Power of God protects me, The Presence of God watches over me, wherever I am, God is, and all is well. Amen."

My Shield

"Lord God, please surround me with favor as with a shield today. Lord, please strengthen your wall of protection around me, keeping me safe from temptation of the flesh, tricks of the adversary, and all harm. Lord, please fill my thoughts with your thoughts and let my words be your words. You are my strength, my shield and my defense, O Lord. Thank you, Lord, in Jesus name I pray, Amen."

Closing Prayer

"In the name of Jesus Christ, I command all human spirits to be bound to the confines of this location. I command all inhuman spirits to go where Jesus Christ tells you to go, for it is He who commands you. Amen"

"God bless every corner of this house, may peace dwell within. Protect all that come and go, whether friend or kin. Bless every door and window pane and every ceiling and wall. Bless every closet, nook and cranny, crawl space, or basement, bless it all. Bless the roof and ground surrounding with your protective love and light. Hold us in your loving care every second of every day, in every way from early morning into sheltered night. Let all be in your complete perfection as you intended. Release all negativity into your confirmed light that is extended. We thank you and expect your miraculous intervention. Clearing all with purification, love, peace, and joy as divinely intended."

Notes